Ten Oxford Authors:
Ten Literary Walks

Edited by

John Mair with
Richard Lance Keeble and
Peter Tickler

Maps: Sebastian Ballard

Published by Bite-Sized Books Ltd 2022
©John Mair 2022

Bite-Sized Books Ltd 8th Floor, 20 St. Andrews Street, London EC4A 3AY, UK

Registered in the UK. Company Registration No: 9395379

ISBN: 9798410620567

The moral right of John Mair to be identified as the author of this work has been asserted by him in accordance with the Copyright, Designs and Patents Act 1988

Although the publisher, editors and authors have used reasonable care in preparing this book, the information it contains is distributed as is and without warranties of any kind. This book is not intended as legal, financial, social or technical advice and not all recommendations may be suitable for your situation. Professional advisors should be consulted as needed. Neither the publisher nor the author shall be liable for any costs, expenses or damages resulting from use of or reliance on the information contained in this book.

Contents

Acknowledgements	1
Editors	2
Introduction	3
Walk One	4

    'Morseland': A Literary Walk, by John Mair and Heidi Boon Rickard, editors

Walk Two	12

    An Oxford Walk with Adam Fawley, by Cara Hunter, writer

Walk Three	19

    Philip Pullman's Lyra's Oxford Walk, by Mark Davies, local Oxford historian

Walk Four	24

    Harry Potter and Oxford: A Literary Walk Round Some Filming Locations, by John Mair

Walk Five	30

    C. S. Lewis, J. R. R. Tolkien and the Inklings, by Peter Tickler, writer

Walk Six	35

    P. D. James, the 'Queen of Crime', and Oxford, by Peter Tickler

Walk Seven	41

    Iris Murdoch: Dreaming of More Than Oxford's Spires, by Professor Gary Browning

Walk Eight   49
    Lawrence of Arabia's Oxford, by John Mair
Walk Nine   54
    'Alice's Adventures in Oxford' Walk, by Mark Davies
Walk Ten   63
    A Walkabout Through the Oxford of Vera Brittain – Nurse, Writer, Feminist and Pacifist, by Anne Manuel, archivist, Somerville College
Walk Eleven   69
    D. I. Holden/Peter Tickler's Murderous Oxford, by Peter Tickler
Appendix   75

Acknowledgements

None of my now 45 books could have been achieved without the hard work of my contributors. All bar one unpaid. They now number getting on for 600. This book is no exception. The individual essays are the backbone. The essayists deserve huge praise. More than them, so does my long-time colleague and friend Professor Richard Lance Keeble. He really is the 'super-sub'. Any loose copy, grammar or punctuation does not escape his (well-read) pen! He turns sow's ears into silken purses in short order. Even the authors appreciate it.

Thanks to all of them and to my publishers who have birthed this book from my dream to your reality in eight short weeks.

John Mair
Oxford, England,
January 2022

Editors

John Mair is the editor of 45 'hackademic' books in the last decade. They mix the work of journos and academics. During the last year, he has edited and published mini-series on *Is the BBC in Peril?* and on the UK covid pandemic, a large volume on *Populism, the Pandemic and the Media,* and most recently *Morse, Lewis, Endeavour and Oxford: Celebrating 35 Years on Screen.* He is published by Bite-Sized Books and Abramis Academic. He has lived in Oxford for 25 years.

Richard Lance Keeble is Professor of Journalism at the University of Lincoln and Honorary Professor at Liverpool Hope University. He has written and edited 45 books on a wide range of media-related topics. Chair of The Orwell Society (2013-2020), he edited *Orwell Today* (2012) and *George Orwell Now!* (2015) and he is the author of *Orwell's Moustache* (2021). He is emeritus editor of *Ethical Space: The International Journal of Communication Ethic* which he launched in 2003, and joint editor of *George Orwell Studies.* In 2011, he gained a National Teaching Fellowship, the highest award for teachers in higher education in the UK, and in 2014 he was given a Lifetime Achievement Award by the Association for Journalism Education. He is a member of Louth Male Voice Choir, Louth Film Club and (through thick and thin) Nottinghamshire County Cricket Club.

Peter Tickler has lived much of his life in Oxford, both as a student at Keble College and as a dweller of Grandpont. As an established crime writer, he has set all of his seven novels in contemporary Oxford. His 'Blood in Oxford' series has been praised for the authenticity of his Oxford ('He has a wonderful gift of creating geographically factual settings for his fictional characters' – *Oxford Times*) as well as the pace of his stories ('deliciously thrilling and wildly unpredictable' – *Oxford Today*). His non-fiction book, *The Modern Mercenary,* was a major success both sides of the Atlantic. He wrote a series of biblical monologues for BBC Radio Oxford, and now teaches creative writing for Oxfordshire Adult Learning. He is a member of the Crime Writers' Association.

Introduction

John Mair

This book is a cornucopia, a bran tub to dip into for those with an interest in good writing from Oxford or further afield. Ten 'authors' with strong Oxford connections are featured. They vary from the nineteenth to the twenty-first century, from fictional characters like Lyra, Morse, Alice, Detective Inspectors Adam Fawley and Holden to real people such as Lawrence of Arabia/Oxford, Iris Murdoch, Vera Brittain and P. D. James.

You, the reader, can explore them and their work through the simple device of a short walk around 'their' Oxford – real or imagined. This is a guide book designed to be taken like tablets one at a time to allow you to soak in the author or their character. All the literary tours are self-guided though, for those with a special interest, there are many professional guided tours of Oxford.

The eagle-eyed will spot an eleventh author – Peter Tickler who has in recent years used Oxford 'town' (not 'gown') as the base for his own brand of detective fiction. He deserves recognition.

The city has been the petri dish for much intellectual activity over the last millennium. Literature to the fore. Do use this guide extensively and do enjoy your walks with a purpose.

Walk One

'Morseland': A Literary Walk

Heidi Boon Rickard and John Mair

Distance: 0.65 miles

Start: Broad Street

End: Turl Street

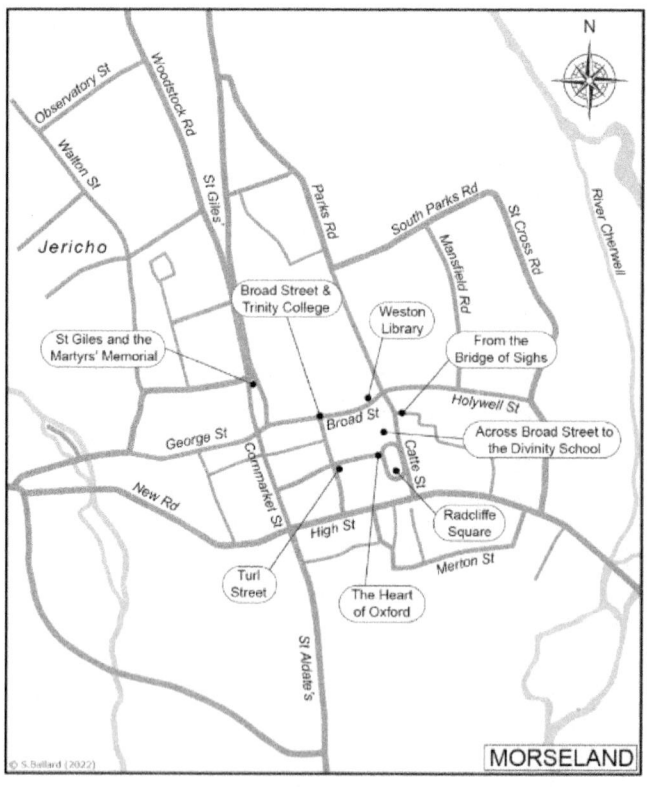

Your guide, Heidi Boon Rickard, is THE *Morse* guide in Oxford. Her Walking Tours of Oxford are regularly packed out. John Mair is her fellow editor.

Inspector Morse is Oxford and Oxford is Inspector Morse. For 35 years, *Morse* and its sequel and prequel – *Lewis* and *Endeavour* – have graced television screens worldwide. They put Oxford firmly on the map. Here, in an abridged version of *Morse, Lewis, Endeavour and Oxford; Celebrating 35 Years on Screen* (Bite-Sized Books, 2021) we take a tour of central Oxford's 'Morseland'.

1. Broad Street, Trinity College, OX1 3BH

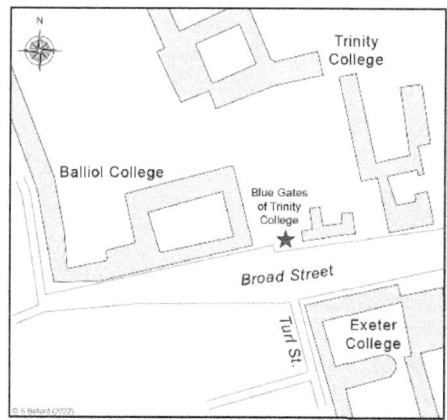

One of my favourite spots as there is so much to talk about here. With the Blue Gates of Trinity behind you, look to the opposite side of the road. Café Itali'Amo (today it has a brilliant secret garden: do explore it) was formerly called Morton's and it appears in the *Lewis* episode, 'Reputation'.

We see Lewis and Hathaway go there to buy their lunch; they cross over and stand talking at the Blue Gates of Trinity. Blackwell's art and poster store is where, in the *Lewis* episode 'Music to Die for', Valli Helm works. She places the advertisement in the paper at the start of the episode which reads 'E. Morse, forever remembered, Love W.'. In many of the *Lewis* episodes, we have a reference taking us back to *Morse*.

Continue along Broad Street passing The White Horse pub on your left. (Note the back and white chalkboard advertising Morse links.). Continue until you reach the Weston Library and across the road is Hertford College and the Bridge of Sighs.

2. Hertford College and the Bridge of Sighs, OX1 3BW

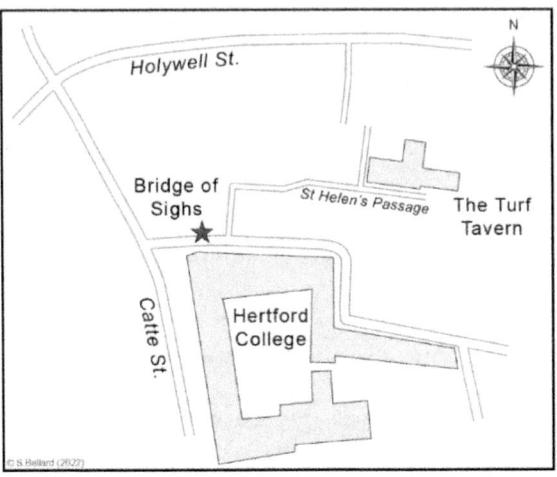

The Bridge of Sighs was designed by Thomas Graham Jackson to connect the two sides of Hertford College. You can see the date by looking up to see the year marked – 1913, which is new by Oxford standards. This area – the bridge and New College Lane – is used many times in the three TV series. As also is New College, the entrance to which is located further along New College Lane. This dates from 1379.

As you look under the Bridge of Sighs, to the left between the stone and brick walls, you should notice a small alleyway which is 'St Helen's Passage'. If you walk down here you come to The Turf Tavern, which is one of the oldest pubs in Oxford and located in the old city ditch. In the *Morse* episode 'Service of All the Dead', Morse, ever partial to a pretty lady, takes a fancy to Ruth Rawlinson who is a suspect in the case. Morse asks her out for a drink, but she declines. That same evening, Lewis and Morse walk into The Turf Tavern and Lewis asks his boss what he would like to drink. Morse sees Ruth Rawlinson having a drink with a man, becomes a little agitated and so refuses the drink from Lewis – virtually unheard of!

Before moving on from this spot, swing around to admire the view, looking back at the Sheldonian Theatre and the other side of the Clarendon Building. It was here, as a procession exits through the Clarendon Building, where Gladys Probert, a Welsh opera singer, is shot in the *Morse* episode, 'Twilight of the Gods'. All the dignitaries are then detained in the Sheldonian Theatre.

This location is also recognisable from the *Endeavour* episode, 'Harvest', in which a CND protestor 'Nigel Warren' preaches at the start of the episode. We see him again later when Thursday and Endeavour come to talk to him about hitching a lift five years ago with a Dr Matthew Laxman. It is in this *Endeavour* episode when Shelia Hancock, John Thaw's widow, has a role.

Continue walking along Catte Street and turn right into Old School's Quadrangle. Position yourself by the statue straight ahead.

3.   Across Broad Street to the Divinity School, OX1 3BG

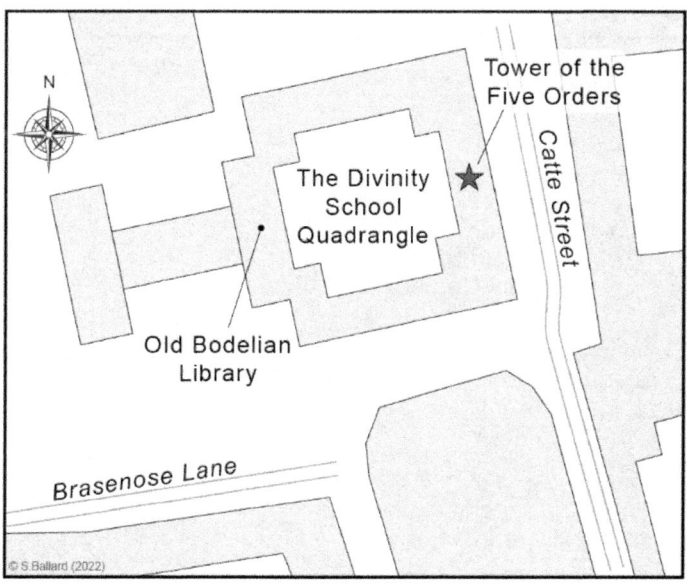

The statue here is of William Herbert, 3rd Earl of Pembroke (1580-1630), Chancellor of the University when this area was built in the 17th century. You will see above the archway, the Tower of Five Orders, the columns on either side representing the five orders of architecture: Tuscan, Doric, Ionic, Corinthian and Composite. Straight ahead of you (opposite the tower and behind the statue) is the entrance to the Divinity School. This is worth a visit: you may recognise it from the *Harry Potter* movies. Above the Divinity School is the Duke Humphrey's Library, the oldest reading room of the Bodleian Library, named after Humphrey of Lancaster (1390-1447), younger son of King Henry IV.

It is not an easy location for filming as it is often very busy. All the same, Morse strides across this area in various episodes and the library's interior has also been used in a number of episodes.

From here, take the left-hand side of the square and wander around looking at these beautiful buildings. When you reach the far side, turn left and stop just by Brasenose Lane.

4. **'The Heart of Oxford', OX1 4EL**

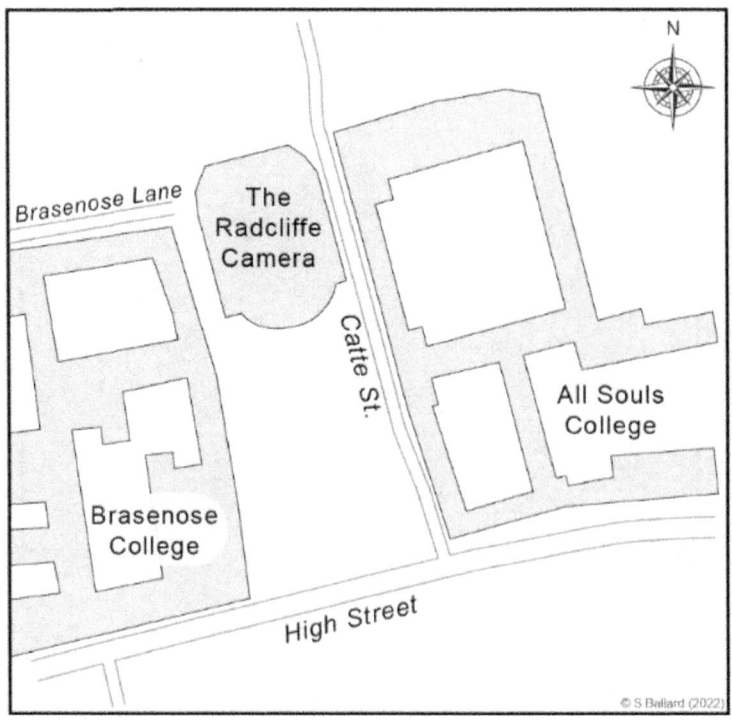

One of the most iconic parts of Oxford, Radcliffe Square is dominated by the Radcliffe Camera. It is used frequently in the filming of the three series. Look around, there is very little to date this area so it can easily be turned back to the 1960s/1970s for *Endeavour*.

We have passed what many consider to be 'the heart of Oxford' as you walked round Radcliffe Square and the Camera. On your left you passed All Souls College which is for research fellows only. It was here where Sir Jeremy Morse (1928-2016) was an honorary fellow and the namesake of our Morse. Colin Dexter loved crossword puzzles and this is a characteristic that he bestowed upon Morse. Colin was also a great admirer of Sir Jeremy and that is how our Morse acquired his name.

At the end of the square, you will see the University Church of St Mary the Virgin, which was adopted as the university's first building – with its congregation meeting here since at least 1252. We would suggest a visit inside.

We next pass the entrance to Brasenose College, founded in 1509, notable alumni including the author of *The Lord of Flies* and winner of the Nobel Prize in Literature in 1983, William Golding, the *Monty Python* actor-cum-travel writer, Michael Palin, and the former British Prime Minister, David Cameron.

It commands a stunning location right in the heart of Oxford and from the front quad there are great views of the top of the Radcliffe Camera. The name of the college comes from its Brazen Nose door knocker: the original hangs behind High Table in the hall but a replica can be seen at the top of the door where the stone meets the wood.

Continue up Brasenose Lane. You will be passing the side of Brasenose College on your left which turns into the side of Lincoln College. Behind the wall on your right is the Fellows' Garden of Exeter College. When you reach the top, turn left and position yourself on the corner of Brasenose Lane and Turl Street.

5.   Turl Street, OX1 3DP

Turl Street has been used many times in the filming of the three series. From your location, you can see three colleges – Lincoln College is behind you (where the post box is), on the opposite side and to your left is Jesus College. Opposite Jesus College, off Turl Street, is the entrance to Exeter College which is the important one here although all are equally beautiful!

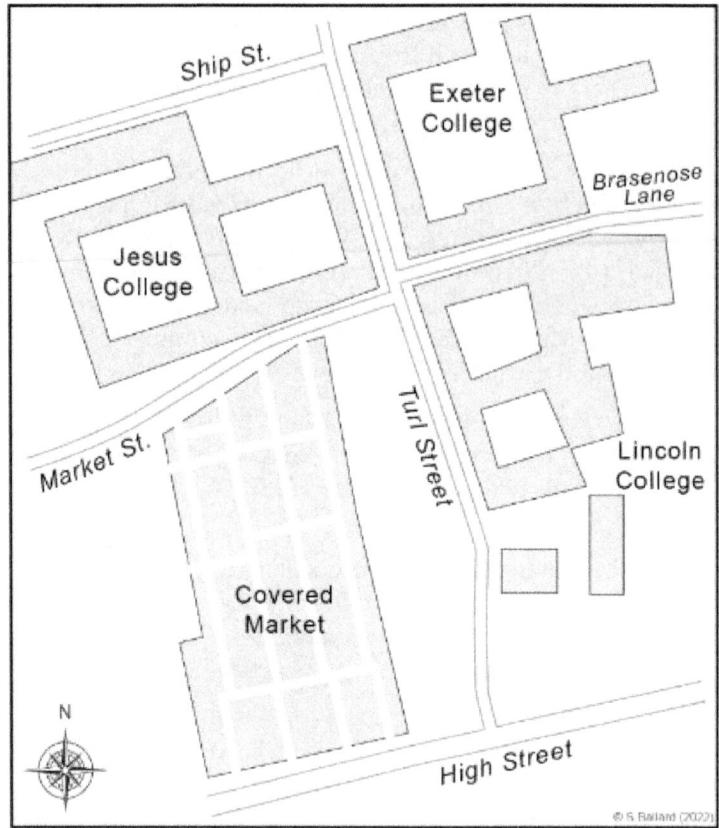

Exeter College was founded in 1314 by the Bishop of Exeter. Notable alumni include J. R. R. Tolkien, author of *Lord of the Rings*, who was a student here (although he also taught at Pembroke and Merton colleges). Exeter is often open to the public between 2-5pm. There is a small charge to enter but is worth it to enjoy an overview of an Oxford college. Especially for anyone keen on *Morse, Lewis* and *Endeavour* for it is one of the most-used college locations for filming.

No *Morse, Lewis* and *Endeavour* tour would be complete without a mention of the last *Inspector Morse*, aired on 15 November 2000. John Thaw died on 21 February 2002. Colin Dexter had written in his will that nobody else should ever play Morse but we have been lucky with the portrayal of the young Endeavour Morse by Shaun Evans who, given the shoes he had to fill, in my opinion has done a magnificent job.

Do go into Exeter College if you are able to and as you walk around the front quad and perhaps take a seat in the chapel, take a moment to think of our Morse, John Thaw and Colin Dexter with 'The Remorseful Day' in your mind.

In the very last *Inspector Morse*, John Thaw goes into Exeter College via the front door. He takes a telephone call from the porter's lodge and then goes into the chapel via front quad. He sits and listens to Gabriel Fauré's ethereal *Requiem* for a few minutes before returning to the front quad. It is here where he has his fatal heart attack. He is taken to the John Radcliffe Hospital where he dies.

Morse ended at episode 33 as did *Lewis*; with three episodes in 2021 of *Endeavour* that brought us neatly to 33. Will this be the end of *Endeavour* or is a new series planned?

Watch your screens.

> An extract from ***Morse, Lewis, Endeavour and Oxford: Celebrating 35 Years on Screen***, edited by **John Mair with Heidi Boon Rickard and Richard Lance Keeble. Available on Amazon and in Oxford bookstores.**

Walk Two

An Oxford Walk with Adam Fawley

Cara Hunter

The Adam Fawley detective novels have sold over a million copies across the world since the publication of *Close to Home* in 2017. Two of the books have been Richard and Judy Book Club picks and the TV rights to the series have been acquired by the Fremantle group. The series is set in Oxford.

Distance: approximately 2 miles
Start: Pitt Rivers Museum
End: Oxford Canal

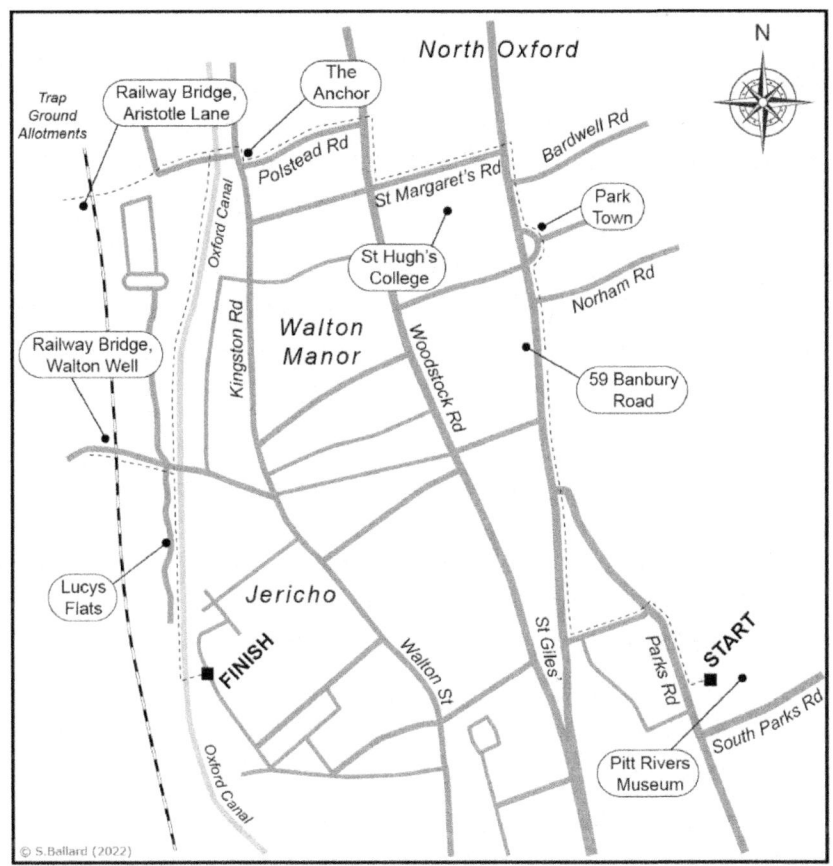

1   The Pitt Rivers Museum South Parks Road, OX1 3PP

One of my favourite Oxford places. In *Close to Home*, Daisy and her schoolmates visit the museum, and her brother Leo becomes enthralled with some of the artefacts.

> There are African shields and Inuit skins hanging under the ceiling and the floor before them is a maze of glass display cases, crammed with every conceivable type of human artefact – *Musical Instruments, Masks, Featherwork and Beadwork, Funerary Boats, Weapons and Armour, Pottery, Coiled Baskets*. So far, so organized, but inside each case is a glorious chaos of dates and places of origin, with Samurai jumbled with Surinam, and Melanesia with Mesopotamia. Some items still have their original labels – minuscule

> Victorian handwriting on yellowing paper attached with string.
> www.prm.ox.ac.uk

From the Pitt Rivers, turn right and head north, skirting the University Parks. Cross to the Banbury Road and continue heading north.

2   59 Banbury Road, OX2 6PE

Once a private house, now owned by Hertford College, this is a classic North Oxford Victorian Gothic building. In *No Way Out*, I make it into the Institute of Social and Cultural Anthropology (which is actually a few doors down).

> A converted Victorian townhouse – as so many smaller Oxford departments are – rising four storeys above a lower ground. Dirty 'Oxford yellow' brick with ornamental woodwork in dark red paint. A bike rack, gravel greened with weeds, two industrial-sized recycling bins and a sign saying no parking.
>
> 'Bloody hell,' says Quinn, pushing the car door shut and looking up. 'You wouldn't catch me working in there. It's like something out of Hammer House of Horror.'

From here keep walking north, passing the turning for Norham Road on the right. This is the sort of road where Michael Esmond and his family live in *No Way Out*. As Fawley observes: 'Round here, houses are divided into large, small, large-small and small-large. Safe to say this is large. *Large*-large.'

3   Park Town, OX2 6SN

This Georgian enclave is one of the jewels of North Oxford, and often featured in both *Morse* and *Endeavour*. In *In the Dark* I rename it Crescent Square, and it's where Rob and Hannah Gardiner have their flat. In the novel, William Harper's large Victorian house in the fictional Frampton Road backs on to the north side of the crescent.

From here, head north a short way, passing the turning for Bardwell Road, where you'll see the signpost for the Cherwell Boathouse, not just my favourite Oxford restaurant but Adam Fawley's too (he talks about taking

Alex there at the end of *No Way Out*). Immediately after that turn left down St Margaret's Road.

4 St Hugh's College, St Margaret's Road, OX2 6LE

This is the inspiration for the fictional Edith Launceleve College in *The Whole Truth*. St Hugh's was originally an all-female college, like its fictional counterpart, but the rest of EL's past and all of its present are definitely my invention!

> Edith Launceleve College – EL to its students – sits on fourteen gardened acres straddling the Banbury and Woodstock Roads. Not very far from town, according to any normal notion of geography, but still the equivalent of Outer Mongolia in the excitable microcosm that is the University of Oxford. EL's splendid isolation from town and all its temptations was no doubt seen as an advantage by its uncompromising foundress, but it's definitely a downside these days – when the University has open days they have to resort to chalk-marks on the pavement to tempt sixth-formers that far north.

At the junction with the Woodstock Road turn right, and then take the first left down Polstead Road. This is where I imagine the Dawsons living in *Close to Home*:

> Four storeys, including a lower ground, and even from where Everett is standing she can see two of the rooms upstairs are lined with books. The front is weathered red brick and recently renovated stone, and there's a line of black railings above a low wall and a neatly gravelled drive. The street is lined with trees that must have been planted when the houses were built, more than a century before.

Go to the end of Polstead, to the junction of Kingston Road.

5 The Anchor Pub, Hayfield Road, OX2 6TT

This is where Adam meets Bryan Gow in *In the Dark*, when Gow is competing in a pub quiz.

It used to be a dingy spit-and-sawdust for the workers at the coal wharf but in the last couple of years it's gone gastro glam. Log fires in winter, shades of paint in grey and teal, black-and-white floor tiles carefully restored.

Alex loves it, and the beer's still good too.

Now take the small bridge opposite the pub and cross the Oxford canal into Aristotle Lane.

This is the area where Daisy Mason's family live in *Close to Home*.

Keep going straight on past the Recreation Ground and go up onto the bridge over the railway.

6   The Railway Bridge, Aristotle Lane, OX2 6UA

This is a new bridge, and when I was writing *Close to Home* the old one was still standing. In the novel, I made the demolition and replacement of the bridge a big part of the plot, and had no idea that there were plans to do exactly that.

It was rather spooky to see life imitating art a year or so later!

From the bridge you can see the Trap Grounds allotments, mentioned in the book, and Port Meadow, which is searched by the police when Daisy goes missing.

Gifted to the city by Alfred the Great, and never cultivated, it's a fabulous and often atmospheric place for a walk.

> Ahead, the old village of Binsey is just visible amid the trees; behind me the towers of the city; to the north, much further away, a smudge of brown that marks Wolvercote. And to the right, closer than any of them, the roofs of Canal Manor, one or two windows catching the sun. Out on the meadow, the mist is still clinging in the hollows and the cattle are moving slowly through the tufts of grass, their ears flicking at unseen midges. And above it all, a huge sky billowed with pinkish clouds.

Retrace your steps now, and at the end of the Rec, take the path down onto the towpath. Turn right and head south towards the city. This is a really pretty walk.

7   The Railway Bridge at Walton Well, OX2 6ED

Come up to road level at the next bridge you come to, turn left and the railway bridge is a short distance away.

This is the bridge where a Network Rail engineering crew see a body fall on to the line in *The Whole Truth,* and this is where the police later source CCTV from a residential building, showing a car leaving the scene.

> The camera is from one of the flats on the corner of William Lucy Way, looking straight at Walton Well Road. The bridge is out of range to the left, but you can see anything – and anyone – heading towards it. Including the car that passes at speed at 01:09 on Tuesday 10th July, fifteen minutes before a team of Network Rail engineers will spot a body falling onto the northbound line.

Go back down to the towpath and turn right, continuing towards the city centre.

8   Lucy's Flats, OX2 6ED

Immediately opposite you now is the new housing development where Gareth Quinn lives in the novels. It's on the site of the old ironworks, which finally closed in 2005.

> His flat is on the top floor, with a view that would justify even an estate agent's hyperbole.

Continue south from here, and if you come off the towpath at the next footbridge you can explore Jericho too.

Note on the Contributor

Cara Hunter is the author of *The Sunday Times* best-selling crime novels featuring D. I. Adam Fawley and his Oxford-based police team. Her books have sold over a million copies in the UK alone, and been translated into 25 languages so far. Her third novel, *No Way Out,* was selected by *The Sunday Times* as one of the 100 best crime novels since 1945. Her first novel, *Close to Home,* sold over half a million copies, was a Richard and Judy Book Club pick and was shortlisted for Crime Book of the Year in the British Book

Awards 2019. The fifth book, *The Whole Truth,* was a Richard and Judy summer pick for 2021. The TV rights to the series have been acquired by the Fremantle group.

Walk Three

Philip Pullman's Lyra's Oxford Walk

Mark Davies

Distance: approximately 2 miles
Start: Botanic Garden
End: Walton Well Road

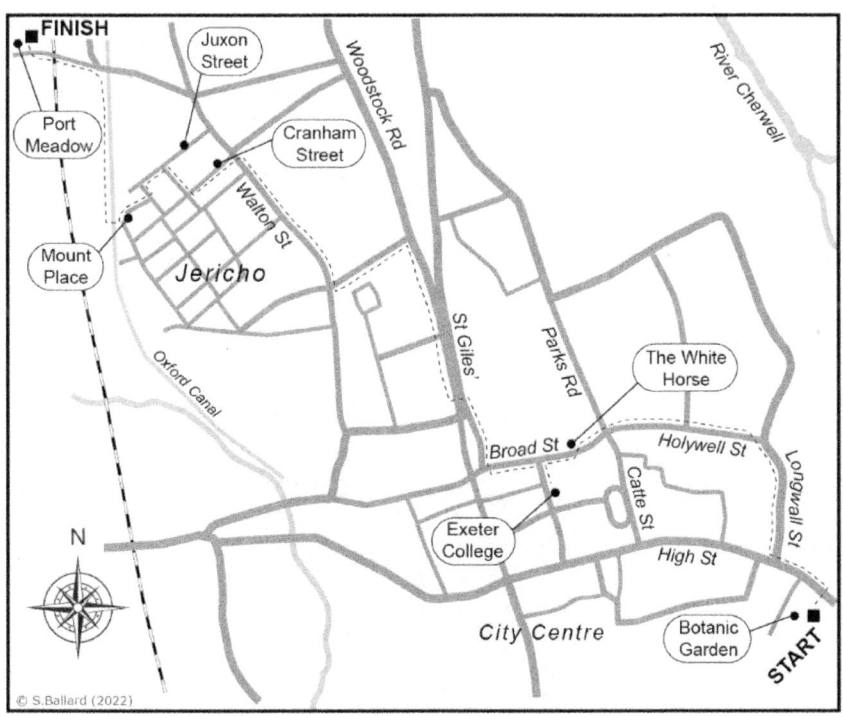

1.   Botanic Garden, OX1 4AZ

This walk begins at the end – the end of the third book of Philip Pullman's first trilogy. For, in 'The Botanic Garden', the final chapter of *The Amber*

Spyglass (2000), Lyra and her friend and fellow adventurer, Will, agree to try to meet in their respective parallel worlds at a particular bench in the Botanic Garden every Midsummer's Day at noon. If you want to locate it, go 'almost to the end of the garden, over a little bridge, to a wooden seat under a spreading low-branched tree'.

The garden also features briefly in *La Belle Sauvage* (2017) when the organisation called Oakley Street, very much concerned with Lyra's wellbeing, needs secure drop-off points for the reports of the Oxford academic Hannah Relf (see Jericho section): 'In the Botanic Garden ... a space under a particular thick root inside one of the hothouses was the first left-luggage office.'

The garden continues to be a focus for Oakley Street's activities in *The Secret Commonwealth* (2019), and it is after a disrupted meeting there that Malcolm Polstead realises the importance of making a journey to Asia.

Walk along the High Street and turn right into Longwall Street, as far as Holywell Street. If you continue north for a mile or so, across University Parks, you may find St Sophia's College where Lady Margaret Hall is usually located. This is the college of both Hannah Relf and Lyra, but is too distant for inclusion in this walk – likewise the Museum of Natural History in Parks Road, where Lyra encounters the sinister Sir Charles Latrom – so proceed along Holywell Street into Broad Street.

2. **The White Horse public house, OX1 3BB**

An episode (in *The Secret Commonwealth*) in the public house, which nestles between two entrances to Blackwell's, demonstrates both Lyra's feminist side and her tenuous identification with the more scholarly side of Oxford. Inside, she finds Dick Orchard, grandson of one of the boat-dwelling gyptians who play such a prominent part in Lyra's destiny. Dick buys her a half of beer, which Lyra greets cuttingly with: 'Oh, a half. Thank you for my half-pint, Dick … If I'd know you were short of money, I'd have asked for a glass of water.'

The incident is prefaced with the comment: 'Lyra wasn't gown now: this evening she was town, exclusively.' Lyra's mixed allegiances, as a resident of a university college but with a best friend, Roger, who was a town boy, are established very early on in *Northern Lights* (or *Golden Compass*, in USA, of 1995) within this nod to an Oxford historical reality: 'When the town children attacked a colleger: then all the colleges banded together and went into battle against the townies. This rivalry was hundreds of years old, and very deep and satisfying.'

3. **Exeter College, OX1 3DP**

The entrance to Jordan College, better known as Exeter, is a short distance down Turl Street. Pullman was a student here in the 1960s. As Jordan, it is Lyra's childhood home in *Northern Lights* and features prominently, too, in the short, stand-alone story called *Lyra's Oxford* (2003). Lyra and her dæmon, Pantalaimon, are tricked by a devious witch into going in search of the alchemist Sebastian Makepeace who lives in Jericho. The route they take to reach the suburb which features often in Pullman's scene-setting (and which suggested to him the name 'Jordan') is one we shall also follow for the next stage of the walk.

A right turn at the corner of Balliol College will take you into St Giles. Walk along the left-hand (western) side. On the far side is St John's College, recalled briefly in *The Subtle Knife* (1997) as a place where Lyra and Roger had once climbed the gates to let off some fireworks. Pass by the Eagle and Child public house, renowned as a location where J. R. R. Tolkien and C. S. Lewis used to meet to exchange ideas about their own fantasy fiction.

At the end of Little Clarendon Street, 'that row of fashionable dress shops and chic cafés, where the gilded youth of Lyra's Oxford passed the time', turn right into Walton Street, and past the imposing entrance to Oxford University Press, or, the Fell Press, as it is called in the two-page excerpt from an Oxford tourist guide included in *Lyra's Oxford*. This is one of numerous examples from this guide of a subtle mingling of factual Oxford with Pullman's fantastical version: it was Bishop John Fell (1625-1686) who introduced the fine type moulds from Holland used in the first permanent university printing press in 1669.

Further along Walton Street, past the Jericho Tavern – which is situated more or less in the location of the 17th century (or earlier) Jericho House, from which the name of the suburb derives – turn left into Cranham Street.

4.   Cranham Street, Jericho, OX2 6DD

As well as their association with St Sophia's College, Hannah Relf and Lyra have one other main thing in common: they can both interpret the alethiometer, the instrument which can answer questions for those who know how to read it. For instance, Hannah uses the alethiometer in *La Belle Sauvage* to contact Malcolm Polstead, a boy at the time, at his father's pub of the Trout at Godstow. It is also at Hannah's house in Cranham Street where the adult Malcolm reveals that he and Alice Lonsdale saved Lyra's life on a perilous journey down the River Thames when she was baby.

A right turn into Cranham Terrace will take you to Juxon Street.

5.   Juxon Street, Jericho, OX2 6DJ

The conclusion of Lyra and Pantamailon's night-time walk in *Lyra's Oxford* comes when they locate the alchemist Sebastian Makepeace's house at the bottom end of Juxon Street. Lyra discovers that she has been tricked, but salvation arrives in the form of a self-sacrificing swan – the subtitle of *Lyra's Oxford* is 'Lyra and the Birds'. Makepeace's house backs on to some ironworks, and the Oxford guide book again provides a teasing glimmer of the truth: Juxon Street was once the home of a famous alchemist called Randolph Lucy, whose dæmon was an eagle; the now-vanished Jericho ironworks were in reality known as the Eagle Iron and Brass Works in the mid-19th century, and familiarly as Lucy's in the 20th century.

Makepeace – who 'used to be a Scholar of Merton, till he went mad. Don't know how they managed to tell in that place' – features again in *The Secret Commonwealth*, but it is the nearby Oxford Canal which now demands our attention, as the all-important habitat of the boat-dwelling gyptians. It lies a few steps along Allam Street, then right into Mount Street.

6.   Mount Place, Jericho, OX2 6BJ

Lyra's pugnacious character is apparent early on in *Northern Lights*, in her enthusiasm for fighting with both the children from other colleges and those of the town, but especially with the 'gyptian families, who lived in canal-boats, came and went with the spring and autumn fairs, and were always good for a fight'.

Lyra soon has great reason to be grateful to the gyptians, however, when they rescue her from danger after the disappearance of one of their own children, Billy Costa. The incident occurs during the annual Horse Fair, when Jericho is depicted as the hub of the gyptian activities in Oxford – exactly as it really was for those working on the canal after World War Two, when Jericho became the *de facto* Oxford terminus after the city-centre basin was sold to build Nuffield College.

So it is easy to imagine a *Northern Lights* Jericho where the wharves were 'crowded with narrow boats and butty boats, with traders and travellers, and the wharves along the waterfront in Jericho were bright with gleaming harness and loud with the clop of hooves and clamour of bargaining'. At the time of writing such scenes remain a future possibility, thanks in part to the prominent support that Sir Philip has given to the long campaign to retain a boatyard worthy of the name in Jericho.

The canal towpath in Jericho is where the young Malcolm Polstead first becomes embroiled in Lyra's affairs, when he retrieves an Oakley Street acorn containing an important message. Malcolm had gone to buy some paint from the chandlery for his canoe, La Belle Sauvage, and it seems appropriate to conclude this walk with a view of the river which is central to the *La Belle Sauvage* plot.

Cross to the canal towpath, walk northwards to the ramp up to Walton Well Road and over the railway lines until the wide vista of Port Meadow is visible.

7. Port Meadow from Walton Well Road, OX2 6ED

It is on a quest to provoke the Costa family, with whom Lyra had been feuding 'ever since she could first throw a stone', that Lyra learns of the disappearance of their boy, Billy. They are in Oxford for the annual Horse Fair on Port Meadow, another example of Pullmanesque pseudo-reality: Port Meadow is where Oxford's historical horse races were held most summers for two hundred years. There is realism, too, in Pullman's allusion – reflecting true historical assumptions about working boatmen – to the gyptians' supposed light-fingeredness and licentiousness, the Oxford guide noting that during the July Horse Fair many 'small objects vanish from unguarded windowsills' and that 'more children are born in Oxford in April than in any other month'.

At the top of Port Meadow is the key location in *La Belle Sauvage*: 'the priory of Godstow, where the gentle nuns went about their holy business; and on the opposite bank from the priory there was an inn called the Trout'. With the baby Lyra on one side of the river and the landlord's son Malcolm Polstead on the other, their adventures are primed to begin. This walk, however, now ends – although, should you be so inclined, it is a simple matter to continue across Port Meadow and follow the Thames Path northwards in pursuit of adventures of your own.

Note on the Contributor

Mark Davies is an Oxford local historian, author, publisher and guide with a particular interest in the history and literature of the city's waterways, having lived on a canal boat in central Oxford for nearly 30 years. He is on the committee of the Alliance of Literary Societies and is the current chair of the Jericho Living Heritage Trust. His current books are *A Towpath Walk in Oxford; Alice in Waterland; Alice's Oxford on Foot; Stories of Oxford Castle, What a Liberty!* and *King of all Balloons.* www.oxfordwaterwalks.co.uk.

Walk Four

Harry Potter and Oxford: A Literary Walk Round Some Filming Locations

John Mair

Distance: 0.8 miles
Start: Christ Church
End: New College

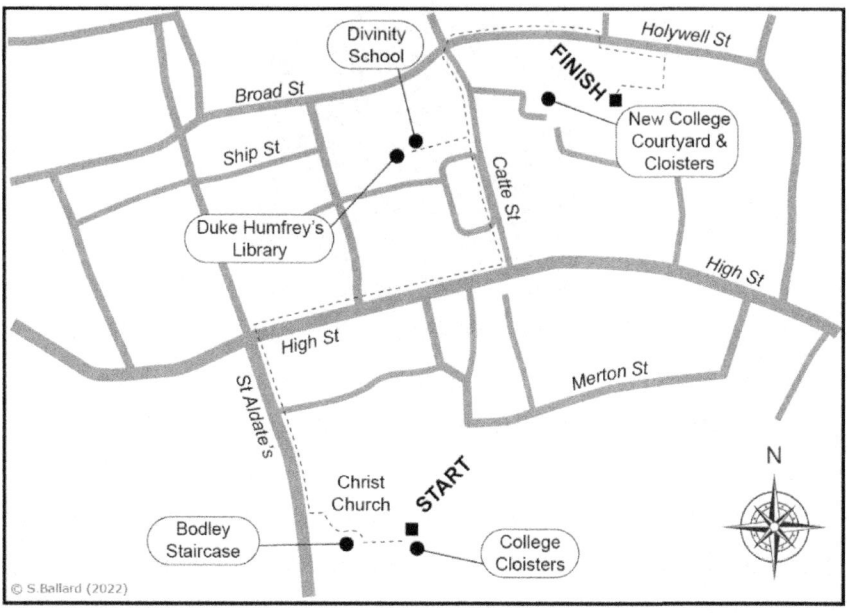

Harry Potter is a great work of children's/adult fiction. No specific connection but many of the scenes in the films were shot using Oxford settings. They form the basis of this walk. You will have to use your imagination or refer back to the films.

Harry Potter was filmed in the following Oxford locations:
- Christ Church – Bodley Staircase
- Christ Church Hall
- Christ Church Cloisters
- Bodleian Library – Divinity School
- Bodleian Library – Duke Humfrey's Library
- New College Cloisters
- New College Courtyard and Tree

1. **Bodley Staircase, Christ Church, St Aldate's, OX1 I DP**

The Bodley staircase leads up to Christ Church Hall. The top of the staircase is used in *Harry Potter and the Philosopher's Stone* when the new first years (including our favourite trio Harry, Ron and Hermione) walk up to Hogwarts for the first time and are welcomed by Professor McGonagall. We also see them return to this spot at the end of the film after they have defeated Professor Quirinus Quirrell and Voldemort and are about to head home.

The bottom of the stairs is used in *Harry Potter and the Chamber of Secrets* – both as the spot where Harry and Ron are collared by Argus Filch after their escapade with the flying car and also where Harry meets Tom Riddle.

- Watch the clip: First Glimpse of Hogwarts Hall in *Harry Potter and the Philosopher's Stone* – https://www.youtube.com/watch?v=SafKm0tsSOw

2. **Christ Church Cloisters, St Aldate's, OX1 IDP**

There are a lot of Christ Church Oxford Harry Potter sites! This one is a little more tucked away than the others. Again, it's from *The Philosopher's Stone* – the location where Hermione shows Harry that he was born to be a seeker – showing him all the trophies that James Potter won during his time in Hogwarts too.

Fee for entering Christ Church: £8-£10

Go north up St Aldate's and Cornmarket. Turn right at Waterstone's bookshop. You are in Broad Street. Go to the end. Opposite the Weston Library you will find a route past the Sheldonian to the Divinity School.

3. **The Divinity School, The Bodleian Library, Broad Street, OX1 3BG**

The Bodleian Library's gorgeous Divinity School is another spot where Oxford University and Harry Potter meet. It was used as a filming location in *Harry Potter and the Philosopher's Stone* and in subsequent films as the Hogwarts Infirmary.

Can you remember that scene in the *Philosopher's Stone* when Harry is recovering after his first encounter with Voldemort and Dumbledore comes to visit him? Or when Harry and Hermione use the time turner leaving poor Ron in the hospital bed in *Harry Potter and the Prisoner of Azkaban*? Can you imagine the hospital beds lined up along the walls with young Harry lying in bed after his first big confrontation with Voldemort?

The Divinity School not only features as Hogwarts Hospital, it makes an appearance in *Harry Potter and the Goblet of Fire* as the hall in which the students practise their Triwizard Tournament dances. Who knew that all that awkwardness (Ron's face when he has to hold McGonagall's waist is just classic) took place in such a beautiful location?

Fee for entering the Divinity School, but only as part of a tour: £2

- Watch the clip: Harry has a chat with Dumbledore while recovering in the infirmary – see https://www.youtube.com/watch?v=jM3dRKpRots

4. **The Bodleian Library, Duke Humfrey's Library, OX1 3BG**

Remember when Harry walked through the Hogwarts library hidden underneath his invisibility cloak with the intention to steal a book: this scene was filmed in the Duke Humfrey's Library, part of the Bodleian Libraries and is only accessible with a private tour. Duke Humfrey's Library also makes an appearance in *Harry Potter and the Philosopher's Stone* in the scene where Harry is wearing the invisibility cloak and looking for information in the restricted section of Hogwarts Library. Yep, you guessed it – that's Duke Humphrey's Library.

Fee for entering Duke Humfrey's Library, but only as part of a tour: £6

Leave the Divinity School square. Turn left past Hertford College. Holywell Street is on your right. Follow that to New College.

5. **New College – Cloisters, Holywell Street, OX1 3BN**

It's a short walk from the Bodleian Library to New College which could easily double up as Hogwarts with its arched stone tunnels and imposing architecture.

Don't let the name fool you – the 'New' College actually dates back to the 14th century.

What a discovery – the gloomily quiet cloisters are one of new secret spots in Oxford. That's great – but where do they pop up in Harry Potter? Actually, they crop up in *Harry Potter and the Goblet of Fire* quite a few times – they were used for many of the corridor scenes, including the one where Harry has to push through all the Gryffindor students wearing Potter stinks badges to go and speak to Cedric.

6. New College – Courtyard and Tree, Holywell Street, OX1 3BN

The New College Courtyard was also used as a location in *Harry Potter and the Goblet of Fire*. 'Mad-Eye' Moody has popped up on the scene and transfigures Malfoy into a ferret and stuffs him down his buddy's trousers before he's told off by Professor McGonagall. Harry comes face to face with Malfoy who is sitting on a gigantic oak tree and Malfoy is then turned into a ferret by 'Mad-Eye' Moody. This particular tree nestles in New College.

Fee for entering New College: £5 in the summer, free in winter

- Watch the clip: 'Mad Eye' turns Draco into a Ferret (serves him right too), *Harry Potter and the Goblet of Fire* – Alastor Moody v.s. Draco Malfoy (HD) https://www.youtube.com/watch?v=HobPkv5TELA

Harry Potter Oxford Locations Map

Here's a map of all the Harry Potter locations:
https://www.google.com/maps/d/u/0/viewer?mid=1dZkCx2wzisY6TAfeEoFbfkwHFBVFeAMV&ll=51.75215781091103%2C-1.2537618500000014&z=16

Sources

Insider's Oxford: insiders@oxford.com

Experience Oxfordshire: www.experienceoxfordshire.org

Walk Five

C. S. Lewis, J. R. R. Tolkien and the Inklings

Peter Tickler

The Inklings were a group of men who from the early 1930s to 1949 formed an informal literary discussion group in Oxford. The best-known members are C. S. Lewis (author of the Narnia series of books, including The Lion, the Witch and the Wardrobe*) and J. R. R. Tolkien (author of* The Lord of the Rings *trilogy).*

Distance: approximately 1.5 miles

Start: Magdalen College, High Street

End: Eagle and Child or Lamb & Flag, St Giles

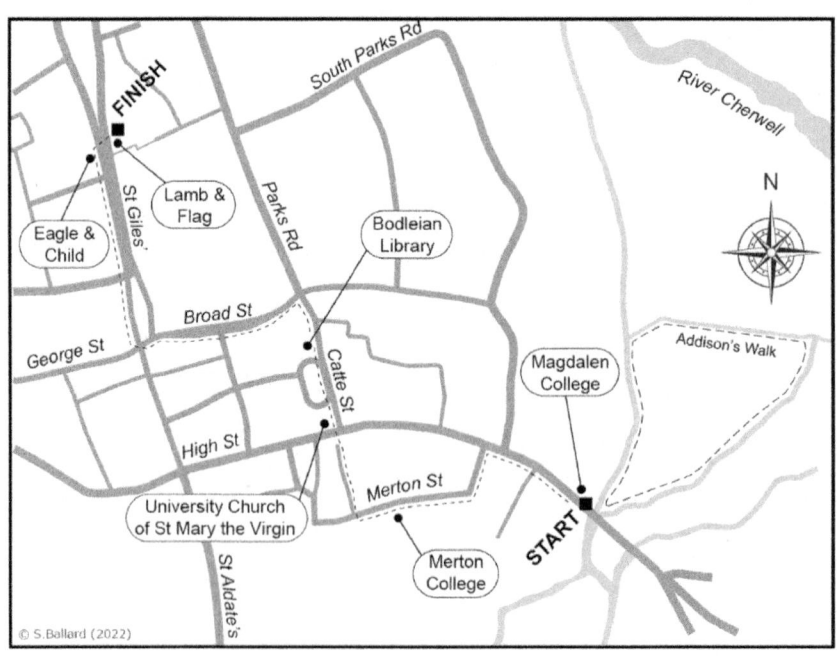

1   Magdalen College, High Street, OX2 6BG

C. S. Lewis was a Fellow at Magdalen College (pronounced 'maudlin') from 1925 until 1954. It was in his college rooms that on Thursday evenings in term time he and fellow members of the Inklings met to discuss literature and also read pieces of their own writing. (See also below under 'The Eagle and Child and Lamb & Flag'.)

Magdalen is fortunate to a have a deer park within its vicinity, and this is surrounded by Addison's Walk. This lovely circular walk was of great significance to Lewis. It was there, one evening, that he had a long discussion with J. R. R. Tolkien about the meaning and power of stories. Tolkien urged his friend to consider the gospel story of Jesus Christ. He argued that this story was the underlying truth to which all other stories pointed and encouraged Lewis to study the facts of Jesus's resurrection.

Lewis was later to acknowledge that it was this conversation which brought him back to the Christian faith. He subsequently wrote several books about Christianity and, of course, also the *Chronicles of Narnia*, in which the lion, Aslan, represents the sacrificial Jesus who then rises to life.

Lewis also wrote a poem about Addison's Walk. It begins: 'I heard in Addison's Walk a bird sing clear:/This year the summer will come true. This year. This year.' The poem in full may be found on a plaque on Addison's Walk.

2   Merton College, Merton Street, OX1 4JD

Tolkien and Lewis first met here in 1926 at an English Faculty meeting. First impressions were not entirely positive. Lewis described Tolkien in his diary as a 'smooth, pale, fluent little chap', but then noted that there was 'no harm in him: only needs a smack or so'.

Despite this, the two men went on to become firm friends and leading lights in the Inklings, where they were greatly encouraged in their writing of fantasy. Tolkien, of course, created a whole complicated fantasy world for *The Hobbit* (1937) and his *Lord of the Rings* trilogy (1956-1957) which formed the basis for a series of blockbuster films directed by Peter Jackson between 2001 and 2003. Tolkien had a lifelong academic fascination with language, and invented more than one of his own Elvish languages.

In 1945, Tolkien became the Merton Professor of English Language and Literature and a Fellow of Merton College, a post he held until 1959. Later, in 1972, he was appointed a Commander of the Order of the British Empire by Queen Elizabeth II.

3   The University Church of St Mary the Virgin, High Street, OX1 4BJ

Turn left out of Merton, then first right up Magpie Lane and you will soon reach High Street. Immediately opposite you across the road stands the University Church of St Mary the Virgin. Apart from being magnificent place of worship, it represents a significant milestone in Lewis's Christian life. On 8 June 1941, at a time of huge anxiety and uncertainty in the country, Lewis delivered a hugely influential sermon entitled *The Weight of Glory*. In this he explored the concept of heavenly glory. It was later published with a number of his other sermons and is generally regarded as a key work.

Access to the church is still free, but if you wish to go up the 127 steps of the tower, you will need to book in advance. The tower is the oldest part of the church (*c.*1280) and you will also pass the Clore Old Library as you ascend to the top from where you may enjoy a splendid view of the city.

Back down on the ground, you may like to try out the Vaults café, either inside or outside on the edge of Radcliffe Square.

4   The Bodleian Library, OX1 3BG

Immediately north of St Mary's is the Bodleian Library. Amongst the many literary treasures which it contains (alongside millions of books, of course) are the illustrations which Tolkien created for *The Hobbit* (see https://tolkien.bodleian.ox.ac.uk).

Tolkien drew a number of maps of Middle-earth. When his publisher Allen and Unwin commissioned the illustrator Pauline Baynes to paint a map of Middle-earth, she worked from the maps which Tolkien provided (1969).

The last two stops on our journey are public houses in St Giles. Walk west along Broad Street, then due north up St Giles, and on your left you will find the Eagle and Child.

5 The Eagle and Child, 49 St Giles, OX1 3LU

This pub (more colloquially known by locals and students as the 'Bird and Babe') stands on the western side of the St Giles. It has acquired worldwide fame because it was here that on a Tuesday lunchtime (during the university term) members of the Inklings would often meet up to chat and read out pieces of their latest stories. They did so in a private lounge at the back known as the 'Rabbit Room'. These informal meetings continued long after the Inklings as a formal group had closed down.

It was here, in 1950, that C. S. Lewis distributed to his friends the proofs of the book which was destined to become a hugely loved bestseller – *The Lion, The Witch and The Wardrobe.*

Lewis continued to meet with other fellow writers at the Eagle and Child until his death in 1963, but Tolkien stopped coming at the end of the 1950s.

- At the time of writing (January 2022), the Eagle and Child is undergoing major refurbishment. It is not clear when it will be open to the public again as a pub and hotel.

6 The Lamb & Flag, OX1 3JS

However, you may wish to visit the Lamb & Flag across the other side of St Giles. This pub, also, has had a difficult recent history, but the Inklings Group, a Community Interest Company, has signed a contract with St John's College to run it on a long-term basis.

The Lamb & Flag is another pub at which members of the Inklings met informally and it, therefore rightly, has a place at the end of our tour. It remains a free house (that is, not tied to any brewery) and will continue to serve a range of real ales, many from local beers. Try a pint to refresh yourself at the end of your walk and toast the wonderful creativity of the Inklings.

Finally ... The Kilns, Lewis Close, Headington, OX3 8JD

For many years Lewis lived with his brother, Warren, close to Oxford, but too far away to include in this walk. However, for those who are interested, the house in Risinghurst/Headington can be visited by arrangement (https://www.cslewis.org/ourprograms/thekilns/kilnstour/). Although a substantial amount of the gardens was sold for housing redevelopment, sufficient of it remains to enable the visitor to see what pleasure and inspiration Lewis gained from it.

Lewis also regularly attended church services at Holy Trinity Church (https://www.hthq.uk/c-s-lewis/), Headington Quarry, less than a mile's walk away, although now across the dual carriageway of the Oxford ring road. Apparently, it was while attending a service one Sunday, he allowed his mind to wander during the sermon and, by the time he had returned to the Kilns for lunch, he had a clear idea for a book that he was to call *The Screwtape Letters* (1942). Featuring a senior devil who gives advice to his nephew on how to bring a human over to Satan's side, it is dedicated to J. R. R. Tolkien.

All in all, the church is well worth a visit. You may see Lewis's grave (he died on the same day, 22 November 1963, that President Kennedy was assassinated), admire the Narnia window and see the location of his favourite seat (https://www.hthq.uk/c-s-lewis/).

Walk Six

P. D. James, the 'Queen of Crime', and Oxford

Peter Tickler

P. D. James (3 August 1920-27 November 2014) was one of the foremost English crime writers of the twentieth century. She became known as the 'Queen of Crime', taking over that unofficial mantle from Agatha Christie. She was born and died in Oxford.

Distance: approximately 2 miles

Start: Leckford Road

End: St Stephen's House

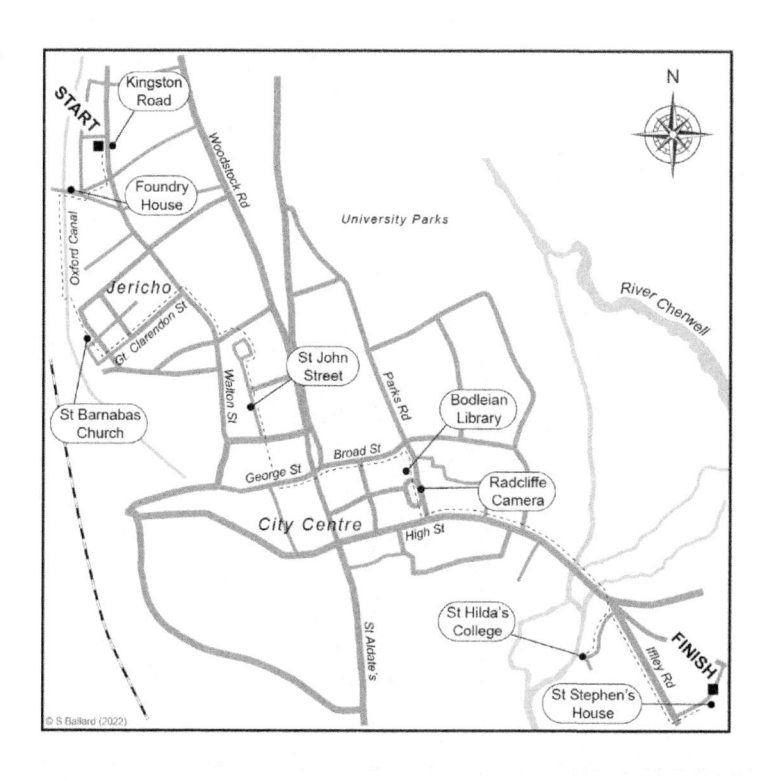

1   164 Kingston Road, OX2 6RP

Born Phyllis Dorothy James and later honoured as Baroness James of Holland Park, the crime writer P. D. James was born in 1920 in Oxford. She lived for a short time in a white house on the corner of Leckford Road and Kingston Road, just on the northern edge of Jericho. Despite the family moving to Ludlow, a market town in Shropshire, by the time she was of school age, this short period in Oxford clearly left an impression on her. Her earliest outings in the pram would have taken her down Longworth Road immediately opposite their house, into Walton Well Road and over the canal and railway into the green expanse of Port Meadow, much beloved by townspeople and students alike, and well worth a stroll. Port Meadow was to feature later in her life, too.

2   88 Foundry House, Walton Well Road, OX2 6AQ

One of the curiosities of James's life is that, despite living much of it in London (notably in a house in Holland Park Road, in west London, on which there is a blue plaque in her name), her last home was only a few hundred metres as the crow flies from her first home. When Lucy's ironworks were redeveloped in around 2010, she bought 88 Foundry House – one of the new flats. This penthouse apartment, quite apart from being more suitable for her needs in old age, also afforded her a view across Port Meadow which gave her very great pleasure.

Perhaps the best view of the flats is to be gained by cutting down from Walton Well Road on to the towpath on the western side of the canal and turning south towards the city. Look up and you can imagine James enjoying the view, ruminating on new writing ideas or playing Scrabble with her friends (something she very much enjoyed). If you continue south on the towpath, past the narrowboats which line the banks, you will eventually reach Hythe Bridge Street, but to continue our trail, you need to turn left across the across the first bridge you encounter into Mount Place. This will take you back across to the eastern side of the canal. Turn right down Canal Street, and you will soon find yourself outside one of James's favourite Oxford places.

3   St Barnabas Church, Cardigan Street, OX2 6BG

James had a close attachment to St Barnabas Church. She attended services regularly whenever she was in Oxford and when it ran a fund-raising campaign for the church she was an active supporter.

The building stands tall and imposing, a Victorian basilica-style church with a magnificent interior, whose tower dominates Oxford's Jericho – an area once notorious as a red-light district, now better known as a desirable and up-market place to live. The poet laureate, John Betjeman, praised the church in a celebrated poem: 'Good Lord, as the angelus floats down the road/Byzantine St Barnabas, be Thine Abode.'

P. D. James made use of the church in *A Taste for Death,* published in 1986, the same year in which she won the Crime Writers' Association's Silver Dagger. In the opening scene, two men (one of them a former minister of the crown, the other an alcoholic vagrant) are found brutally murdered in St Matthew's Church: 'They lay like butchered animals in a waste of blood.' James did not believe in playing down the violence of murder. But this imagined church of St Matthew's is a thinly disguised St Barnabas Church. It has also (such is the god-like power of the fiction writer) been moved some 60 miles to Paddington, in west London.

Come out of Jericho via Great Clarendon Street, cross over Walton Street to Little Clarendon Street. At the Oxford University Clarendon Building turn right through Park Square to St John Street

4   51 St John Street (off Beaumont Street), OX1 2LQ

James owned No. 51 for a number of years. It was essentially a weekend house, a place to escape to from London, with the advantage of being close to some of her family. But this house, with a basement and four further floors, is important for another reason: it brings us to her only novel set in Oxford.

The Children of Men (1992) is a stand-alone novel, inspired by some alarmist reporting in the press about the diminishing sperm count amongst men. It is set in a dystopian Oxford of 2021. No children have been born for a generation. When protagonist Theo Faren moves a few months after a major trauma in his life, it is to a house in St John Street. The Oxford of her dystopian world is very different from the real Oxford of 2021. Yet the description of Faren's house sounds like No. 51.

This novel was turned into a film of the same name in 2006 (directed by Alfonso Cuarón, and starring Clive Owen and Julianne Moore) which was much praised by the critics. P. D. James herself was pleased with it too, despite the significant changes that any complex novel undergoes when rewritten for the big screen.

Immediately opposite No. 51 is a blue plaque for the painter William Turner, not to be confused with the more famous Joseph Mallord William Turner (1775-1851). William Turner, of Oxford (1789-1862), was primarily a watercolour painter who depicted many rural scenes of the county as well as views of Oxford.

Go down St John Street to Beaumont Street, cross over and walk through Gloucester Green. You come to George Street. Turn left and follow that through to Broad Street to the end and the Bodleian/Weston Library.

5.   The Bodleian Library, OX1 3BG

The next leg of our walk ends at St Hilda's College. But make sure you to get there via Broad Street, walking past Blackwell's bookshop. How many of her books have been sold there?

And who can resist a snoop round inside? Immediately next door is the Weston Library, where the Bodleian's special collections are housed. It also now has a lovely airy and spacious café where you can rest your feet (and have a comfort break).

James was an active supporter of the Bodleian and her book, *Talking About Detective Fiction* (2009), was written specifically as part of a fund-raising campaign for it. There were many calls on her time, yet throughout her life she was an immensely hard worker, famously starting work at 5 a.m. in order to get her first Dalgliesh detective novel written before children and her job called her (*Cover Her Face*, 1962).

Next, head south past the Radcliffe Camera Library, then east down High Street, over Magdalen Bridge before turning right into Cowley Place. At the end of this cul-de-sac, you will come to St Hilda's College.

6. Radcliffe Camera to St Hilda's College, OX4 1DY

James has the extraordinary distinction of being awarded four honorary fellowships, one of them being at St Hilda's. She also gave the conference dinner speech at the very first St Hilda's Mystery and Crime conference in 1994. The topic was women crime writers.

I am not aware that there is any transcript of what she said, but *Talking About Detective Fiction* gives a detailed account of her thoughts on her fellow crime writers. Joyce McLennan, who was James's personal assistant and typed all her novels, told me: 'She had great respect for Agatha Christie, but she certainly didn't see herself as her successor, as her own writing was very different with a strong emphasis on characterisation and a sense of place. With Agatha Christie, the emphasis was on the ingenious puzzle.'

The last stop on our trip is a short walk down Iffley Road. Proceed past the Oxford University track (on your right) where Roger Bannister ran the first four-minute mile on 6 May 1954. A little further on, where the road curves to the right, you will see on your left St Stephen's House, a theological training college in the former monastery of the Society of St John the Evangelist.

7. St Stephen's House, 16 Marston Street, Oxford, OX4 1JX

The St John the Evangelist Church which stands at the front (at 109a Iffley Road, OX4 1EH) is a piece of superb Victorian neo-Gothic, and has also become the SJE arts centre, hosting a wide range of musical and cultural events.

As for its connection with P. D. James, St Stephen's is the model for the similar training college in her novel *Death in Holy Orders* (2001). In this case, she did not transport the building to her preferred murderous location, but she did spend many hours in St Stephen's House researching the working of theological colleges before creating her own one – St Anselm's, which she situated on the coast of east Anglia.

Acknowledgements

The author wishes to thank a number of people who helped in composing this essay, including Marni Graff, Jim White, Joyce McLennan and Elizabeth Sirett. He remains entirely responsible for all its content.

Walk Seven

Iris Murdoch: Dreaming of More Than Oxford's Spires

Gary Browning

Oxford was central to the life of Iris Murdoch. As an undergraduate between 1938-1942, she began studying philosophy and became immersed in the Classics. A Booker Prize winner in 1978, her novels are full of characters like the ones she came across in Oxford: wordy, tortuous professors, domineering intellectuals, powerful women and sidelined children. Oxford was always a part of Iris even if she dreamed beyond its spires.

Distance: 5.25 miles

Start: Corpus Christi College, Merton Street

Finish: Lamb & Flag public house, St Giles

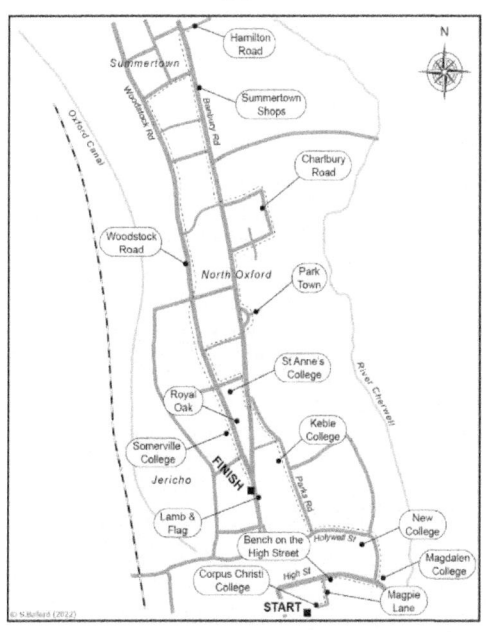

1.   **Corpus Christi College, Merton Street, OX1 4JF**

The Murdoch walk begins at Corpus Christi College, on the wonderful, cobbled Merton Street. In 1940, Murdoch visited Corpus Christi to attend the seminar on Agamemnon, given by the brilliant but demanding Classics scholar, Eduard Fraenkel, a refugee from Nazi Germany. She was reading Classics (Mods and Greats) and her philosophy and novels include many references to the classical world. The good for her was imagined in Platonic terms, and her novels invoke Greek myths and classical paintings.

Walk along Merton Street towards the Eastgate Hotel and to Magpie Lane.

2.   **Magpie Lane, OX1 4ES**

The delightful Magpie Lane joins Merton Street to High Street. In 1939, Murdoch joined the Magpie Players – a group of touring actors who performed ballads and songs – set up by Tom Fletcher, who lived in Magpie Lane. They toured Oxfordshire and Murdoch would retain her love of theatre throughout her life, writing a number of plays including *The Servants and the Snow* (1970) and *The Three Arrows* (1972).

On reaching the High, turn sharp right, where the Quod Restaurant will appear before you.

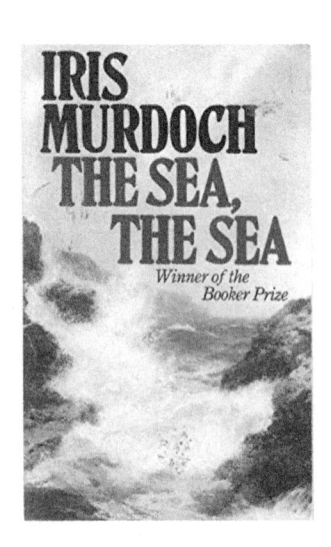

3.   Bench on the High Street, outside Quod, OX1 4BJ

Admire the bench outside Quod Restaurant, which has a plaque commemorating Iris Murdoch. She is one of Oxford's outstanding literary figures; her philosophy is now prized for its critical encounter with preceding orthodoxies and her novels won many awards including the Booker Prize for *The Sea, The Sea* (1978). The gentle curve of High Street contributes to its charm, making it, according to the celebrated architectural historian Nikolaus Pevsner, 'one of the great streets of the world'.

Continue to walk along the High until you reach Magdalen College.

4.   Magdalen College, High Street, OX1 4AU

A grand and imposing college building, its grounds boast both a deer park and the Cherwell River. The marvellous opening scene of Murdoch's late novel The Book and the Brotherhood (1987) is inspired by Magdalen College. At a college ball attended by most of its characters, some of the male characters converse with a Classics professor, modelled on Fraenkel, and after a terrific argument between Duncan Cambus and David Crimond, Cambus ends up in the river. The charismatic but wild Crimond is employed by some of the characters to write a great critique of Western society. The fate of this book, its protracted writing and its wildness, serves as a metaphor for the state of politics and society in the late twentieth century.

From Magdalen College walk along Longwall Street and turn left into Holywell Street until you reach New College, opposite the Holywell Music Room, the oldest concert hall in Europe.

5.   New College, Holywell Street, OX1 3UA

When, in 1956, Murdoch married John Bayley, the Oxford novelist, literary critic and subsequently Professor of Literature, he was a tutor in English at New College, where he had studied as an undergraduate. Iris visited him at the college and sometimes would dine there.

On leaving New College, head towards Parks Road and turn right to go along it, heading towards Keble College.

6.   Keble College, Parks Road, OX1 3PG

Along with Philippa Foot, Murdoch would go to Keble for tutorials in philosophy with the charismatic Donald M. MacKinnon. Murdoch had a close relationship with MacKinnon, yet according to Conradi, Murdoch's biographer, his wife Lois resented Murdoch, and MacKinnon put a stop to things. In Murdoch's early novel *The Sandcastle* (1957), MacKinnon's wife is a likely source of the rather sour character, Nan Mor, wife of the novel's major protagonist, Bill Mor. MacKinnon would write an equivocal reference for Iris when she applied for a fellowship at St Anne's College.

On leaving Keble College, follow the Parks, turn into Banbury Road and then cross Bevington Road into Woodstock Road. Then turn right where you will see St Anne's College.

7.   St Anne's College, Woodstock Road, OX2 6HS

Murdoch became a Fellow in Philosophy at St Anne's College in 1948, holding the fellowship until she resigned in 1963. Her teaching was unorthodox and lively, covering a range of historical, continental and Anglo-American thought. In his interesting memoir of his wife, *Iris* – the basis for the feature film, *Iris*, of 2001, starring Judi Dench, Jim Broadbent and Kate Winslet – John Bayley describes St Anne's at the time he met Iris as a 'hotbed of emotion'.

On leaving St Anne's, go across Canterbury Road and into Banbury Road and then cross the street into Park Town.

8.   Park Town, OX2 6SN

A wonderful crescent of Georgian houses, whose inhabitants have included many dons and literary figures, including Booker Prize-winner Ian McEwan, who references it in his novel, *Solar* (2010). Iris Murdoch lived in Park Town twice: initially as a second-year undergraduate in No. 43, and then again in

1946/7 at No. 16, with Philippa Foot and her husband, the military and intelligence historian, M. R. D. Foot. Philippa was a great friend, but living with the Foots was somewhat awkward as when sharing a flat in London during the war, Murdoch had taken up with Philippa's on-off boyfriend, Thomas Balogh, later to become an eminent economist, and into the bargain had then dumped her own boyfriend, M. R. D. Foot. In truth, Murdoch was deeply troubled over what had happened, and she later wrote movingly to Philippa Foot, expressing deep remorse for her part in it.

Head north from Park Town into Charlbury Road.

9. 30 Charlbury Road, OX2 6UX

Iris and John Bayley lived here from 1988 until the end of Murdoch's life in 1999. Iris would work downstairs in the study on this quiet residential north Oxford road, looking out on to the garden and road. Like previous houses, life here was highly disorganised, with papers, books and sometimes food strewn about the place.

At the end of Charlbury Road and before Oxford High School for girls, turn left on to Banbury Road and walk along to the parade of shops.

10. Summertown Shops, Banbury Road, OX2 7BY

On moving to Summertown in the mid-1980s, Murdoch would remark in a letter to Philippa Foot how she liked to visit these unprepossessing shops.

Head north along the Banbury Road and turn right into Hamilton Road

11. 68 Hamilton Road, OX2 6AY

At the end of 1985, Murdoch and Bayley were finding their grand house in Steeple Aston, a village a few miles north of Oxford, rather too much to maintain. The roof was leaking, rats scurried across floors and chaos reigned. In response, John Bayley bought this modest suburban house. They soon found that it was not to their taste.

On leaving Hamilton Road, turn around and head back along Banbury Road, and turn right into Woodstock Road just before the parade of shops.

12. Woodstock Road, OX2 7NN

This is a long road of commanding houses, built for dons at Oxford University. In October 1938, Murdoch campaigned in the famous 'appeasement' by-election in Oxford for the Popular Front candidate, Sandy Lindsay, against the Conservative candidate, Quintin Hogg. (Though Lindsay lost, he reduced the Conservative majority from 6,645 to 3,434.) She canvassed down the left-hand side of Woodstock Road. Murdoch's commitment to communism would pass, but throughout her life she would retain a strong interest in politics

Head south along Woodstock Road until you reach Somerville College on your right.

13. Somerville College, OX2 6HD

Murdoch came up to Somerville in 1938, taking First-Class honours in 1942. She arrived at the college fresh from being head girl at Badminton School for girls, in Bristol, having lived before that in London and briefly, Dublin. Studying in Oxford during the war had certain advantages because of the absence of many young men from 1939: it allowed young women like Iris Murdoch the opportunity to assume a more prominent place in the university.

Murdoch befriended many people in Oxford: staff and students, including fellow undergraduates, Philippa Foot, Elizabeth Anscombe and Mary Midgley – all of them later becoming eminent philosophers. Foot would help to reshape moral philosophy, Anscombe, a formidable woman, would work closely under Ludwig Wittgenstein and refashion notions of action, while Midgley would widen the scope of philosophy to include concern for animals and the planet. Murdoch shared intellectual ambitions with these friends, notably in critiquing current moral ideas. Yet she was also influenced by continental philosophy and, while becoming a major novelist, would also seek to refashion metaphysics.

More or less opposite Somerville is the public house, the Royal Oak..

14.   The Royal Oak, Woodstock Road, OX2 6HT

Scene of Murdoch's first alcoholic drink, a gin and lime. Murdoch loved pubs and she enjoyed, drinking, smoking and talking in pubs for the rest of her life. She relished visiting pubs in Soho during the war, while she worked by day in the civil service.

After taking in the Royal Oak, carry on into St Giles, and visit another pub on the left-hand side, the Lamb & Flag.

15.   Lamb & Flag, St Giles, OX1 3JS

A famous Oxford pub in which Murdoch would spend time early in 1951 as she was forming a loving relationship with the famous Oxford anthropologist, Franz Steiner. He was one of a number of émigrés who populated the city during and after the war. Murdoch worked with refugees in UNRRA (United Nations Relief and Rehabilitation Administration) at the end of the war, and she retained an interest in migrants and refugees throughout her life.

In Conclusion

Iris Murdoch was a very social person, and in Oxford she formed enduring friendships with influential women, fell in love with Frank Thompson and Franz Steiner amongst others, and met and lived with her husband, John Bayley. If she would kick against the traces of its philosophy, reading Simone de Beauvoir and Jean-Paul Sartre when they were ignored by the university's Establishment, she would always respect the trademark analytical style of Oxford philosophy. Her late and insightful 'Manuscript on Heidegger', in which she relates the German's thinking to analytical philosophy, is now due to be published – at long last.

Note on the Contributor

Gary Browning is Professor of Political Thought at Oxford Brookes University. He lives in Oxford, drinks in its pubs, talks in its cafés and walks its streets. He is the author of many books including *Why Iris Murdoch*

Matters (Bloomsbury, 2018), *A History of Modern Political Thought: The Question of Interpretation* (OUP, 2016), the editor of *Murdoch On Truth and Love*, and co-editor with Constantine Sandis of *Dylan at 80: It Used to Go Like That, and Now It Goes Like This* (Palgrave, 2021). He is the director of the Oxford Brookes' Think Human Festival and is currently writing a book for OUP, *Iris Murdoch and the Political.*

Walk Eight

Lawrence of Arabia's Oxford

John Mair

Distance: 2.8 miles
Start: Magdalen College
End: Polstead Road

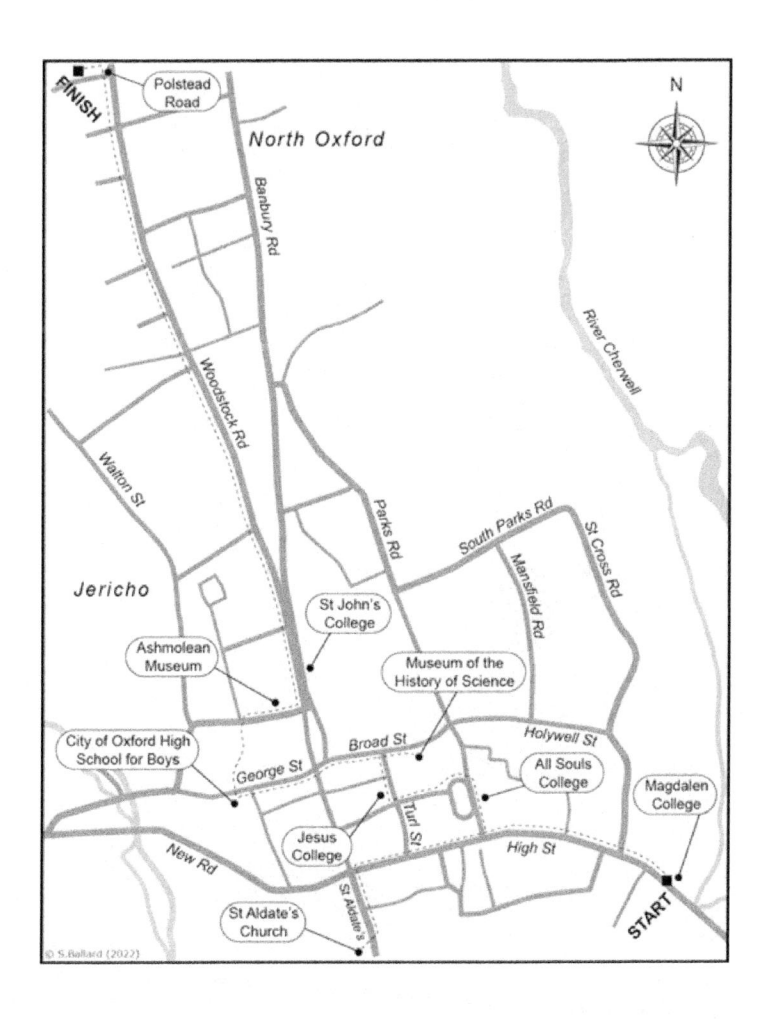

T. E. Lawrence is best-known as Lawrence of Arabia, the author of the autobiography, *Seven Pillars of Wisdom*, and the subject of the multi-Oscar-winning David Lean film in 1962. But he could equally be seen as 'Lawrence of Oxford'. His connections to the City of Spires are very strong. Brought up in the city, he went to school here – and to the university too.

Seven Pillars of Wisdom had an uneven genesis. First drafted in 1919, this version was first lost/stolen at Reading rail station, then burnt (bar one page) by the author, before a third, reconstructed version was published in a limited edition in 1926, then wider by Jonathan Cape in 1927 before becoming a best-seller (50,000 copies sold) after Lawrence's death in a motorcycle accident in 1935. It is considered one of the great pieces of reportage of the twentieth century.

1.   Magdalen College, High Street, OX1 4AU

Lawrence has strong links here. The college gave him a fellowship – the Senior Demyship – in 1910. That gave him four years at £100 per year and offered Lawrence the chance to go to Carchemish, in Syria, for an archaeological dig and there develop his already extant interest in the Middle East. His mentor, D. G. Hogarth, the Keeper of the Ashmolean Museum, put him up for it. His other referees included the Principal of Jesus College and Sir Ernest Barker, the political scientist then at St John's College.

Having gone to the Middle East he never really left it until after the 1916-1918 Arab Revolt and the battles described in *Seven Pillars*. Lawrence returned to Oxford just briefly in 1922, 1923 and 1924. His Magdalen and other Oxford connections served him well in the Middle East as archaeologist, soldier, diplomat and spy.

Lawrence's archive is held at Magdalen College as is that of his authorised biographer Jeremy Wilson. There is also a bust of Lawrence in the college, created by Eric Kennington and donated by Michael and Felicia Crystal, alumni of the college. Magdalen staged a well-received exhibition 'Lawrence of Oxford' in 2018 detailing all his Oxford connections and the many writings by and about him.

Voluntary diversion up 'the High' to Carfax Tower and then turn left into St Aldate's.

2.   St Aldate's Church, St Aldate's, OX1 1BT

Evangelical Christianity was an important influence in Lawrence's upbringing. The Lawrence family attended services at St Aldate's, opposite the main entrance to Christ Church. Lawrence took an active part in the life of the church, helping to run its branch of the Church Lads' Brigade and teaching in its Sunday School.

If diversion not taken, walk along the High Street – known as 'The High' in university circles – from Magdalen to St Mary's, the university church; then turn right and walk through Radcliffe Square to All Souls College on your right.

3. All Souls College, OX1 4AL

In 1919, Lawrence was elected to a seven-year research fellowship at All Souls. The college was founded in 1438 and is primarily an academic research institution with no undergraduate members. Election as a fellow provided Lawrence with an income while he worked on *Seven Pillars of Wisdom.* He had rooms in the college but spent most of his time elsewhere. Mention of his fellowship appears prominently on the headstone of his grave in Moreton, Dorset.

All Souls College has a collection of Lawrence memorabilia including the gold dagger he sold to Lionel Curtis for £125 to pay for repairs at his cottage, Clouds Hill. It also holds a bronze bust of Lawrence sculpted (from memory) in 1946 by Lady Kathleen Scott, widow of Scott of the Antarctic, and presented to All Souls after her death.

From All Souls cross Radcliffe Square to Turl Street, turn right and you will find Jesus College on your right.

4. Jesus College, Turl Street, OX1 3DW

Lawrence applied for a history scholarship at St John's College, which had already accepted Bob, his elder brother. He then turned to Jesus College which had special awards open only to men with Welsh connections. Although he had no Welsh ancestry, he had been born in what was then Caernarvonshire and this enabled him, in 1907, to be elected to a Meyricke Exhibition with an annual value of £40.

Lawrence's undergraduate degree in history was taken here from 1906-1909. He was a brilliant student who, not surprisingly, was awarded a First-Class Honours. His long vacations were taken up with a 2,000-mile cycle tour of France in 1908 and a 1,000-mile walking tour of Syria in 1909. That bore fruit in his undergraduate dissertation on 'The Influence of the Crusades on European Military Architecture – To the End of the 12th century', complete with hand-drawn illustrations. Maps were a lifelong obsession with Lawrence.

From Jesus go up Turl Street towards Broad Street. Blackwell's music shop is on your right. Turn right: the Museum of the History of Science is on the right just in front of the Sheldonian Theatre.

5. Museum of the History of Science, Broad Street, OX1 3AZ

Lawrence was a keen photographer, a skill learned from his father. Between 1911 and 1914 he was responsible for photography at the British Museum's Carchemish excavations in Syria. The Museum of the History of Science, in Broad Street, holds the camera that Lawrence used at Carchemish and also his father's camera.

Turn around head towards Waterstones bookshop. Cross the road to George Street. Go west along that until you come to New Inn Hall Street on the left. The next building on your left is the Oxford University History Faculty building. That is our sixth stop.

6. City of Oxford High School for Boys, George Street, OX1 2RL

Lawrence and his four brothers attended school here. It was a newly-opened grammar school, low in fees but with a high reputation, which provided a sound classical education and had excellent links to the nearby university colleges. 'Ned Lawrence', as he was known, was at the school from 1896 to 1907. The building in George Street is a substantial and highly ornate design evoking the best of Victorian extravagant architecture

Lawrence was a star pupil garnering prizes. He often plumped for history books about Egypt and the Levant. His 'spare time' was not wasted. Lawrence and his schoolfriend Cyril Beeson cycled around Berkshire, Buckinghamshire and Oxfordshire, visiting almost every village's parish church, studying their monuments and antiquities, and making rubbings of their monumental brasses. In 1908, they went on a tour of Crusader castles in Brittany, France.

The building is now part of the university's History Faculty and is not open to the public, but in appearance from the outside it is much as Lawrence would have remembered.

A bronze plaque carved by Eric Kennington, depicting Lawrence surrounded by images reflecting his different interests throughout his life, is hung on the wall of the staircase, alongside a memorial to the fallen of the First World War, including his brothers Will and Frank.

In George Street cross the road, past the Odeon, go through Gloucester Green to Beaumont Street. When you find the Oxford Playhouse, the Ashmolean is across the road.

7. The Ashmolean Museum, Beaumont Street, OX1 2PH

Lawrence's mentor, A. G. Hogarth, was the Keeper here from 1909 to 1927. As a schoolboy 'Ned' searched the building sites of Oxford for archaeologically interesting objects including wine bottles of local companies. The Ashmolean's *Annual Report* for 1906 said that the two teenage boys (Lawrence and Beeson) 'by incessant watchfulness secured everything of antiquarian value which has been found'.

The Ashmolean holds some important portraits and drawings of Lawrence by Augustus John and William Roberts, as well as John's portrait of Feisal, who had fought alongside Lawrence in the Great Arab Revolt and later became King of Syria and King of Iraq, used on the cover of the first edition of *Seven Pillars of Wisdom*. Various other works and objects associated with Lawrence in its collection include some of his brass rubbings, Arab robes and the carved doors he brought back from Jidda, Saudi Arabia, after a visit in 1921

Turn left out of the Ashmolean to St Giles. St John's College is across the road by the Lamb & Flag public house.

8. St John's College, St Giles, Oxford, OX1 3JP

While Lawrence was at university, some of his tutorials were with Ernest Barker at St John's. He was also familiar with the college because two of his brothers, Bob and Will, were undergraduates there.

From St John's College turn right: go up Woodstock Road for about a mile. Polstead Road is on the left just after St Margaret's Road.

9. The Family Home 1896-1921, 2 Polstead Road, OX2 6TN

His family back story was 'interesting'. He was born out of wedlock in August 1888 to Sarah Junner (1861-1959), a governess, and Sir Thomas Chapman, 7th Baronet (1846-1919), an Anglo-Irish nobleman. Chapman left his wife and family in Ireland to cohabit with Junner. Chapman and Junner called themselves Mr and Mrs Lawrence, using the surname of Sarah's likely father; her mother had been employed as a servant for a Lawrence family when she became pregnant with Sarah.

There is a blue plaque here. No. 2 Polstead Road is a substantial red-brick, semi-detached house built about 1890. It has four floors including a basement. It stood in what was then a newly-established neighbourhood just to the north of the university colleges. The area was much favoured by professional men and their families, including many university dons taking advantage of the relatively recent abolition of regulations forbidding college fellows to marry.

The Lawrence family moved here in 1896. His father, mother and four brothers lived here with him. This was his home while he was at school and university, and his only proper home until he finally settled at Clouds Hill, in Dorset, in 1923. The small bungalow built for him in the garden still stands, though altered since his time. Lawrence's father died in 1919 and his mother sold 2 Polstead Road in the early 1920s. It is privately owned today and not open to visitors. In 2020, it sold for £2.6m.

Lawrence: Out of Oxford

Dorset

The Lawrence Trail from the Tank Museum at Bovington BH20 6JG

This circular trail starts and finishes at the museum taking in Lawrence of Arabia's last home at Clouds Hill and his last resting place – the cemetery at Moreton.

London

The flat where he wrote Seven Pillars, *14 Barton Street, Westminster, London SW1P 3NE*

Films about Lawrence

1919 Lowell Thomas film (and stage show) *With Allenby in Palestine and Lawrence in Arabia*; 1962 *Lawrence of Arabia*: David Lean's film, starring the dashing Peter O'Toole, was nominated for ten Oscars at the 1963 Academy Awards and won seven including the Best Picture award.

Lawrence and Arabia and After

1910 December, set sail for Beirut; 1911 Carchemish, Syria, dig for four seasons; 1914 Second lieutenant/interpreter; 1914 The Arab Bureau set up in Cairo; 1914 Sent to Negev as a researcher/spy for British military intelligence; 1916-1918 Arab Revolt aided by Lawrence; 1922 Joined the RAF under false name; 1923 Forced out of the RAF; 1923 Joined Royal Tank Corps under the name T. E. Shaw; 1925 Readmitted to the RAF

Sources

'Lawrence of Oxford' 2020 exhibition catalogue, Magdalen College

The T. E. Lawrence Society: https://telsociety.org.uk

Walk Nine

'Alice's Adventures in Oxford' Walk

Mark Davies

Distance: approximately 2 miles
Start: South-west corner of Christ Church Meadow
End: Oxford University Press, Jericho

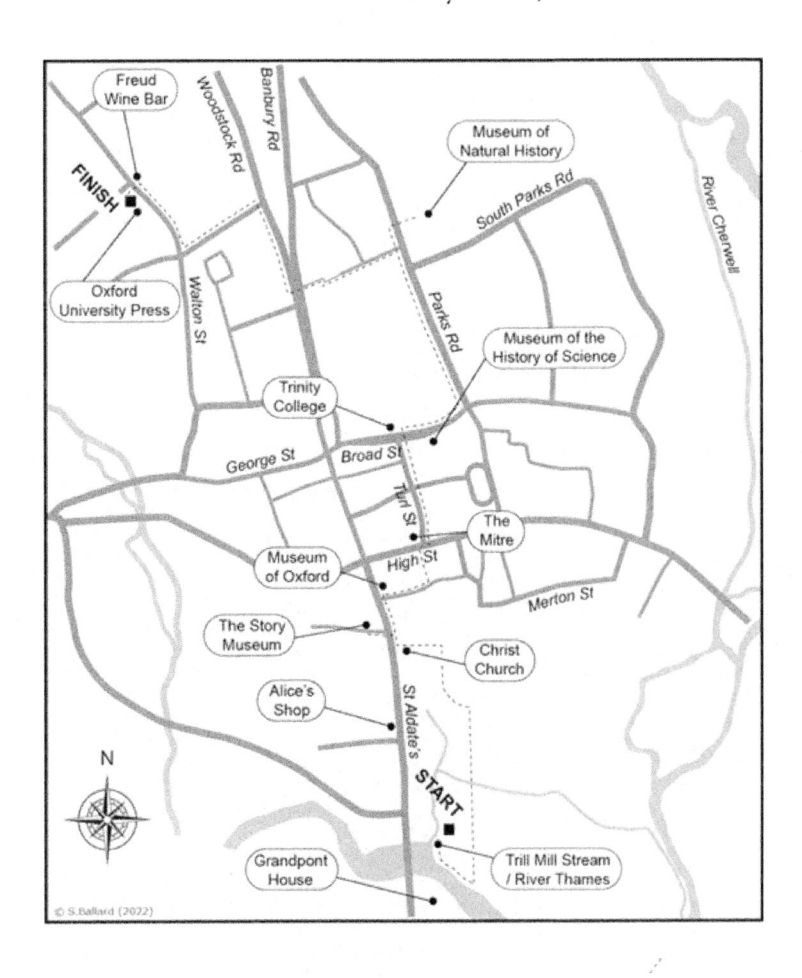

As the King of Hearts once said: 'Begin at the beginning ... and go on till you come to the end. Then stop.' You can stop wherever you like, of course – but as far as the beginning is concerned, probably the most appropriate starting-point is Christ Church, the residence of Charles Lutwidge Dodgson (1832-1898), better known as Lewis Carroll, the author of *Alice's Adventures in Wonderland* (1865). Therefore, contrariwise, and with a dash of down-the-rabbit-hole logic, this walk starts somewhere else.

1. Trill Mill Stream/River Thames Confluence: Christ Church Meadow, OX1 1DP

At the south-west corner of Christ Church Meadow, accessed either through the main gates to the Christ Church Memorial Garden in St Aldate's or the narrow kissing gate near the Head of the River public house, the Trill Mill Stream flows into the River Thames. Dodgson hired rowing boats from here over a period of seven years in the 1850s and 1860s to take the daughters of the Dean of Christ Church, Henry Liddell, on outings up and down the river.

These river outings were fundamental to the creation of *Alice's Adventures* for three main reasons.

Often they would last a whole day, giving Dodgson ample opportunity, bordering on an obligation, to keep Ina, Alice and Edith Liddell amused by inventing impromptu stories on the move; some scenes in the books are clearly based on their actual experiences on the river; and riverside places, people and events inspired some of the characters and episodes. Most importantly, it was on a river trip upstream to Godstow, on 4 July 1862, that the extraordinary phenomenon of 'Alice' was born, when Dodgson agreed to write the story down for Alice Liddell (1852-1934).

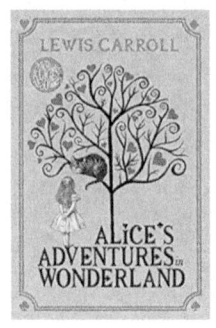

2. Opposite Grandpont House: Christ Church Meadow, OX1 4LD

Walk a short distance downstream and stop where the tree-lined avenue leads to the left. On the opposite side of the river, beyond a metal footbridge, is a three-storey mansion, situated above a side-stream of the Thames. This house was well-known to the real Alice, who recalled in old age: 'A special pleasure was to be allowed to take Rover out for a walk. Rover was a retriever belonging to a well-known Oxford tailor, called Randall, who lived in a house built on arches over the Isis, which he christened Grandpont.' Sure enough, Thomas Randall *was* a tailor, well-known for his prominent High Street shop and many years as a city councillor, but he always called himself a hatter, leading to an increasingly popular idea that Randall was the inspiration for Carroll's Hatter. (The idea was originally my own, I should say, first suggested in 2010 in *Alice in Waterland*.)

3. Christ Church, OX1 1DP

Walk away from the river along the avenue which leads to Christ Church. The view across the Meadow to the right presents a beguiling sense of timelessness, little changed since the days when Dodgson habitually walked here. Often, as we know from his diaries, he did so in company with the Liddell girls and their governess, Mary Prickett (a likely inspiration for the Red Queen).

The visitors' entrance to Christ Church is immediately in front of you at the end of the avenue. By all means go inside, but the history of the college and its association with the world's most famous children's story – no, I don't mean Harry Potter! – are so easily acquired that we shall move on. Suffice to say that this is where Dodgson was an undergraduate, then a lecturer and academic, from 1851 until his death in 1898, and that Alice Liddell lived here from 1855 until her marriage in 1880.

4. Alice's Shop, OX1 1RA

On the opposite (western) side of St Aldate's from the gates of the Christ Church Memorial Gardens is Alice's Shop. This 'little dark shop' has a fair claim to being the one depicted in John Tenniel's illustrations for the 'Wool & Water' chapter in *Through the Looking-Glass* (1872). It is an idea which is strengthened by the sudden transformation from a relatively normal shop to one where Alice and the Sheep are in a rowing boat. Throughout the 19th century this low-lying part of Oxford was subject to floods, so the sight of people resorting to small boats under such circumstances was probably one that denizens of Christ Church observed from their drily elevated sanctuary on a regular basis.

5. **Museum of Oxford, Oxford Town Hall, OX1 1BX**

Walk up St Aldate's as far as Blue Boar Street, noting in passing the rooms at the top corner of the Christ Church façade. These were occupied for many years by Dodgson, who also incorporated a dark room for developing photographs. Inside the Town Hall is the Museum of Oxford, reinvigorated in 2021 after a period of Heritage Lottery-funded refurbishment. Although the museum concentrates on city rather than university topics, Charles Dodgson and Alice Liddell are featured by way of some personal possessions and various items of *Wonderland* memorabilia.

6. **The Story Museum, OX1 1BP**

On the far side of St Aldate's, a short distance along Pembroke Street, is another venue which may justify a detour, The Story Museum, which engages young people through 'imaginative exhibitions and exciting … events … designed to encourage parents, carers and children to spend time together enjoying stories in many different ways'. Alice's story is one of them, of course, and The Story Museum has coordinated Oxford's annual Alice's Day since the first one in 2007.

7. **The Mitre, OX1 4AG**

Turn left out of Blue Boar Street into Alfred Street and cross the High Street into Turl Street. The Mitre (now closed) was run by the Liddell family's governess, Mary Prickett, from 1870 until 1920, initially with her new husband, Charles Foster. There has been an inn at this location since the 13th century and Mary's tenure is the longest known in all that time.

8.   Trinity College, OX1 3BH

At the junction of Turl Street with Broad Street you will see the entrance to Trinity College opposite. This was where Dodgson's friend Robinson Duckworth (1834-1911) was a fellow. Duckworth accompanied Dodgson on several boat trips with the Liddells, most notably on the fateful one to Godstow on 4 July 1862. He was immortalised as the Duck in 'The Pool of Tears', a chapter based on another of their rowing trips on the River Thames.

9.   Museum of the History of Science, OX1 3AZ

A short distance along Broad Street to the right is the Museum of the History of Science. Here you can see the portable case of chemicals that Dodgson used to develop the hundreds of photographs he took during his life. He acquired his first camera in May 1856, and it was while helping a friend to take photographs within Christ Church that year that he first met and spoke to Alice Liddell.

10.   Museum of Natural History, OX1 3PW

Turn left into Parks Road and continue to the Museum of Natural History. This houses the most complete soft-tissue remains anywhere in the world of the extinct bird known as a dodo. Dodgson incorporated a dodo into the 'The Pool of Tears', apparently as a self-mocking reference to the stutter which caused him to pronounce his own name as 'Do-do-Dodgson'.

Walk to the end of Museum Road opposite and through Lamb & Flag Passage into St Giles, noting on the far side the Eagle and Child public house, where two 20th century writers, C. S. Lewis and J. R. R. Tolkien, exchanged ideas about their own fantasy worlds. Cross the Banbury and Woodstock roads at the lights near St Giles Church, and walk down Little Clarendon Street to the junction with Walton Street. Turn right and stop outside the glassily unmissable Blavatnic Building.

11. Freud Wine Bar (formerly St Paul's Church), OX2 6AH

The Freud wine bar was formerly the parish church of the fledgling parish of St Paul's when it was built in the 1830s. Here, Dodgson, an ordained deacon, preached his first-ever sermon in Oxford, on 14 May 1865, to 'the largest congregation I have yet addressed, 300 or 400 I should think'.

12. Oxford University Press, OX2 6DP

Some 2,000 copies of the first edition of *Alice's Adventures in Wonderland* were printed here in 1865 – although, because the famous illustrator John Tenniel was dissatisfied with the quality, this edition was never distributed, making the handful of surviving copies immensely valuable. The ledger detailing the considerable cost of £142 19s 2d paid by Dodgson is on display in the small OUP museum, which can be visited only by appointment. Thomas Combe was the superintendent of the press at this time and lived within the complex with his wife, Martha. Dodgson was a frequent visitor and here, in 1863, he met Alexander Macmillan, who subsequently agreed to publish *Alice*, and also the Pre-Raphaelite sculptor Thomas Woolner, who fatefully influenced Dodgson's decision to engage Tenniel as his illustrator rather than use his own drawings.

That is the end of this walk, although there are many more Oxford locations associated with Alice, so you could easily continue – possibly with my *Alice's Oxford on Foot* (2016 [2014]) to hand. The direction you go next, as the Cheshire Cat would have it, 'depends a good deal on where you want to get to'. See also *Lewis Carroll's Diaries*, edited in ten volumes by Edward Wakeling (1993 to 2007) and *The Annotated Alice*, by Martin Gardner (many editions).

Walk Ten

A Walkabout Through the Oxford of Vera Brittain – Nurse, Writer, Feminist and Pacifist

Vera Brittain (1893-1970) was a writer who rose to fame in 1933 with the publication of *Testament of Youth,* a memoir of her time as a nurse during the First World War. Somerville College's archivist Anne Manuel provides an overview of her life and then takes us on a walking tour of the major sites in Oxford associated with Brittain.

Distance: 2.9 miles

Starts: Somerville College

Ends: Somerville College

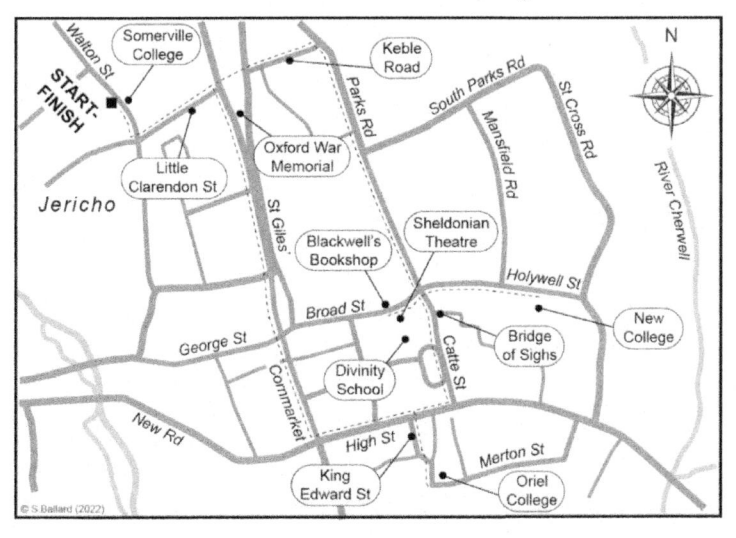

Introduction: A Start in Life

Vera Brittain was born in 1893 and grew up in a prosperous middle-class Victorian household in Derbyshire. Despite the traditional views of her father concerning the role of women, she managed to persuade him to let her try for a place at Oxford University. She was accepted and entered Somerville College in October 1914, two months after the start of the Great War. She was extremely close to her younger brother Edward, who was also due to begin his studies at Oxford that year. However, he was keen to join the war effort as an officer with the 11th Sherwood Foresters and to her subsequent bitter regret, Brittain helped him persuade their father to let him go.

Earlier that year, Brittain had met and fallen in love with Edward's best friend Roland Leighton and they became engaged in 1915, although he, too, was in active service in France for most of that year. Increasingly aware of the devastating nature of the war, fearing for the safety of her brother and fiancé and becoming frustrated with the passivity of the scholastic life, she decided to leave Oxford in June 1915 and train as a nurse. Her worst fears came to pass when she received news in December 1915 that her fiancé had been killed in action.

Over the next three years, two more of her male friends were also killed and finally, in June 1918, her beloved brother, Edward. Her nursing duties had taken her to London, Malta and France and in her final posting she had nursed mainly German soldiers. She had seen the full horror of the casualties, both physical and mental, that had been inflicted upon both sides and these experiences strongly influenced her later pacifism. In May 1919, still grieving deeply for her lost friends and relatives, she returned to Oxford to complete her education. She changed course from English to Modern History in an attempt to understand the origins and nature of the war she had experienced at first hand.

Back at Oxford

Brittain had changed out of all recognition from the young woman who had entered Somerville in 1914. She was now angry, disillusioned and bitter. But she found herself among fellow students who had no experience of what the war had been like for those on the front line, fellow students who were keen to focus on their academic lives and futures. She found it difficult to move on and felt increasingly isolated and disengaged. Her sense of futility of the war and of the deaths of her closest friends deepened. Fortunately, she found an ally in her tutorial partner Winifred Holtby. Holtby had also left college to undertake war work with the Women's Army Auxiliary Corps. They struck up a friendship, drawn together by their shared experiences – and this friendship helped Brittain through the final two years of her studies.

Oxford and Degrees for Women

At this time, the University of Oxford, though allowing women to take the same courses of study and exams as men, did not allow women to become full members of the university nor receive a degree at the end of their studies. This line was becoming increasingly difficult to hold by the end of the war when so many women had kept the university going through their teaching and research. In 1920, the university held a general meeting which paved the way to admit women and, in a ceremony in October of that year, the first degrees were awarded to the heads of the five women's colleges alongside those female students who had passed their exams, sometimes many years earlier. Brittain and Holtby were present at both events and, in turn, were awarded their degrees the following year in 1921.

Testament of Youth

Vera had long held ambitions to become a writer and, moving to London with Holtby, they began their careers, writing novels, short stories and articles for such feminist journals as *Time and Tide*.

They also became heavily involved in the League of Nations, working towards a permanent peace. It was not until 1933, however, that she found the real literary success she had been hoping for with the publication of *Testament of Youth* – an account of her life before, during and just after the war.

The focus was on the despair she felt at the waste of young lives – both those who died and those who survived but were mentally damaged for the rest of their lives – and at the same time on her respect for the sacrifices that her generation had made. It struck a chord with a country facing the possibility of another war and became an instant best-seller.

During the Second World War, Brittain became a vocal pacifist, publishing a newsletter, *Letters to Peace-Lovers*, along with further works condemning blanket bombing and, following the nuclear attacks on Hiroshima and Nagasaki in August 1945, nuclear weapons.

Partly because of this, her popularity dwindled after the war was over though she continued to write and speak, particularly in pacifist and disarmament circles.

In 1925, Brittain married George Catlin, a political scientist (1896-1979). Their daughter, born in 1930, was the Labour cabinet minister, later Liberal Democrat peer, Shirley Williams (1930-2021), one of the 'Gang of Four' Labour rebels who founded the Social Democratic Party in 1981.

When Vera died in 1970, her legacy was in danger of disappearing but in 1979 a republishing of *Testament of Youth* by the feminist publisher Virago, and a subsequent, highly popular TV series adaptation by the BBC in 1979, brought her work back into the public eye. The book has been re-issued many times since then and was the subject of a feature film, directed by James Kent, in 2014 starring Alicia Vikander.

The Literary Walk

1. **Somerville College, Woodstock Road, OX2 6HD**

The walk starts at Somerville College on Woodstock Road where Brittain was admitted as a student in 1914. Continue south towards the city reaching the corner of Woodstock Road and Little Clarendon Street

2. **Little Clarendon Street, OX1 2HS**

End of Little Clarendon Street. where Vera Brittain said goodbye to her brother Edward before he left for active service.

3. **Oxford War Memorial, St Giles, OX1 1DP**

Further down Woodstock Road where it meets St Giles you will see the Oxford War Memorial on the other side of the road.

4. **7 King Edward Street, OX1 4HL**

Keep walking down St Giles, Magdalen Street and Cornmarket for about 1 kilometre until you get to the Carfax tower corner where Cornmarket meets High Street. Turn left along the High Street and after 200 metres turn right into King Edward Street. No. 7, where Vera Brittain first lodged on her return to Oxford after the war, is on the right-hand side

5.   Oriel College, OX1 4EW

Continuing into Oriel Square you come to Oriel College, Somerville College's home between 1915 and 1919.

6.   The Divinity School, OX1 3BG

Retrace your steps to the High Street, cross the road and turn right. After 100 yards turn left into Catte Street passing the Radcliffe Camera. Turn left into the Bodleian quadrangle and right again through the north exit towards the Clarendon Building. The building behind you is the Divinity School where Brittain and Holtby listened to the arguments for and against allowing women to become full members of the university.

7.   The Sheldonian Theatre Broad Street, OX1 3AZ

To1 the left of you is the Sheldonian Theatre where Brittain received her degree in 1921.

8.   The Bridge of Sighs, OX1 3BL

Looking to the right, you will see the Bridge of Sighs, part of Hertford College where Brittain and Holtby first met and had tutorials together.

9.   Blackwell's Bookshop, Broad Street, OX1 3BQ

Continue north to Broad Street and turn left for 50 metres. Opposite is Blackwell's bookshop. Basil Blackwell, son of the founder Benjamin Blackwell, gave Brittain her first paid assignment editing *Oxford Poetry* in 1920. Retrace your steps passing the Weston Library and carry on over the junction into Holywell Street keeping the Kings Arms pub on your left.

10.   New College, Holywell Street, OX1 3BN

Continue for 200 metres to reach New College on your right. This was the college that Brittain's brother Edward was due to attend in 1914 had he not chosen to take a commission with the 11th Sherwood Foresters. It was also where Brittain found solace before and after the war, attending services in the chapel and listening to the choir.

11.   Keble Road, OX1 3QG

Retrace your steps to the Kings Arms junction and turn right up Parks Road. Continue for 700 metres passing the Natural History Museum on your right and Keble College on your left until you get to Keble Road. Turn left into Keble Road – No 8 was where Brittain lived for a year from October 1919 to June 1920. Carry on along Keble Road and cross over Banbury Road by the pedestrian crossing.

12.   Somerville College, Woodstock Road, OX2 6HD

Take the footpath opposite that goes past St Giles Church to emerge on Woodstock Road. Turn right and cross the road to end the walk at Somerville College. On the outside wall of the college you will find a plaque that commemorates the college's role in the First World War as the site of the 3rd Southern General Hospital, including among its patients, the convalescing poets Siegfried Sassoon and Robert Graves.

Note on the Contributor

Dr Anne Manuel is the librarian and archivist of Somerville College, Oxford, home of the largest collection of Vera Brittain material in the UK. She has edited a history of the college *Breaking New Ground: A History of Somerville College as Seen Through its Buildings* (2013) and co-produced the college's latest publication, *Somerville 140, 1879-2019: A Celebration of Somerville College in 140 objects* (2019).

Walk Eleven

D. I. Holden/Peter Tickler's Murderous Oxford

Peter Tickler

In 2006, I started writing my first crime novel, Blood in Oxford *(2008). As a long-time resident of Grandpont in south Oxford, I was determined to write about 'town', not 'gown'. So I wrote about the Oxford I knew and loved rather than the hallowed halls of stone-built Oxford colleges. Seven novels to date. Most feature D. I. Susan Holden.*

Distance: approximately 4.5 miles

Start: Carfax

End: Westgate Centre or Marlborough Road

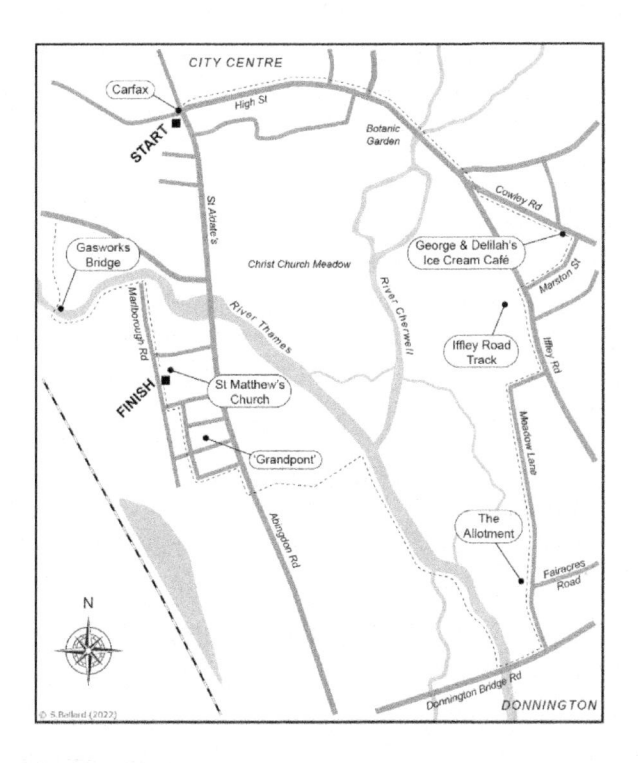

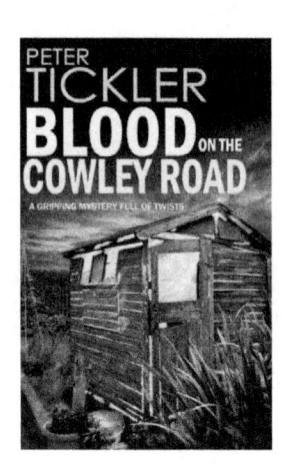

1.   Carfax, OX2 6AY
Cowley Road and the Case of the Moving Car Park

Take your starting point as Carfax, the perfect place to begin if you are coming into the city centre via bus (Oxford has no fewer than five park and rides!). Stroll down High Street, past various colleges, the Examination Schools and the Botanical Gardens. Soon you will be on Magdalen Bridge which, as well as spanning the River Cherwell, acts as a bridge between the two worlds of the old medieval university city and the Victorian and post-Victorian world of east Oxford.

Once over the bridge, there is a choice of three roads, but we will take the middle one, although all three have witnessed startling violence in my books. St Clements, to the left, has a car-park in which one of my characters comes to a nasty end one dark wet night. But we will take the middle road.

You will not need to walk far down Cowley Road before you can look up and imagine what happened at the beginning of *Blood on the Cowley Road*. An old lady crosses the road and is alarmed to hear a terrible scream above her. She imagines it to be a seagull in pain, but then is transfixed when a woman's body falls with a thump on to the pavement in front of her.

I write 'look up and imagine' deliberately – because in reality there is a no multi-storey car-park here. The one I am thinking of, which inspired this unfortunate death, is actually a mile or more away in Between Towns Road,

Cowley. Sometimes as a writer you have to just invent or move buildings from one place to another. And also remember that real people have plunged to their deaths from the real car park in Cowley. May they rest in peace.

2   George and Delilah's Ice Cream Café, OX4 1HP

I love this place. It has been in the Cowley Road, serving the most delicious ice-creams, for many years. And it is here that David, a young man on the behavioural spectrum, comes every lunchtime after eating his sandwiches. Indeed G. & D.'s is a key location in the book because this is where David is approached by a woman who has been stalking him and who had earlier called into the picture-framing shop where he works.

> I always eat it very slowly and I never have the same ice-cream two days running. Yesterday I had pistachio.
>
> And then the woman with the red hair walked in. Her name is Bella. I didn't call her that, of course, because she is a customer. She bought me a passion fruit and mango ice-cream. I shouldn't have agreed to that, but I got flustered, what with her coming in and saying at the top of her voice what an amazing coincidence it was us meeting again, and maybe it was written in the stars. She started to sound really weird ... (*Blood on the Marsh*, 2012).

Walk on (after you've had an ice-cream!) and look around. Cowley Road is multi-cultural and multi-faceted with restaurants and cafés to suit every taste (Thai, Indian, Jamaican, Japanese, Spanish etc.), the much-loved Ultimate Picture Palace, music and bike shops, two mosques, a music venue ... But don't get too distracted. Soon you must turn right down Marston Street and keep going until you reach Iffley Road.

3   Iffley Road Track, OX4 1SR

On the far side of the road is a place of history, the Iffley Road sports ground where Roger Bannister famously ran the first four-minute mile in 1954.

Less famously, it is also the scene of a hit-and-run in *Dead in the Water* (2015). Unfortunately for private detective Doug Mullen (the victim was also his client), most of the inhabitants of Oxford were glued to the TV at this time of night, and the only one who wasn't was an old lady who was standing at the window of her Iffley Road flat, listening out for Tom Tower to strike nine o'clock.

'Well, of course I didn't see anything.'

Mullen tried not to let his disappointment show. 'Not to worry. Maybe …'

The old woman exploded into laughter, rocking back and forth with glee. 'Haven't you noticed?'

Mullen looked at her, nonplussed. What was so funny? And then the penny dropped. 'You're blind!' Suddenly it was glaringly obvious.

'And you claim to be a private eye!'

And while you're here, you may like to consider a recent murder. Oxford historian and art dealer Adrian Greenwood was murdered at his house in Iffley Road on 4 April 2016. The motive was theft of an early, very valuable, edition of Kenneth Grahame's *The Wind in the Willows*, first published in 1908. It sounds like a plot from a Morse novel but, in fact, this really happened. Fortunately, the culprit, Michael Danaher, was soon captured – through a mixture of modern technology and his own stupidity – as highlighted in a Channel 4 documentary, *Catching a Killer*, in 2017.

4   The Allotment, Fairacres Road, OX4 4BJ

Cross the road, and head down Jackdaw Lane. At the end, turn left and walk south, past green space and a primary school, before continuing along Meadow Lane, right past the Fairacres Road allotments in which – you guessed it – another character in *Blood on the Cowley Road* meets a premature and violent death.

He dies in a garden shed on the allotment, but I have since been informed by someone who read my book that this was impossible. Why? Sheds are not allowed there! You see what happens – even when I am trying to describe an authentic Oxford, things *occasionally* go wrong.

The next stretch is the longest part of the walk, but it is surely worth it. When you reach the main road, turn right over Donnington Bridge and then right again down on to the footpath along the western side of the Thames (or Isis as it is known here). Now walk north and enjoy all the pleasures a river can bring, not least the college rowers practising for Torpids (in March) or the Summer Eights (in June). When you reach the University College Boathouse, turn left up a path which leads you to the Abingdon Road and beyond it to Grandpont.

5. Chilswell Road, Grandpont, OX1 4PU

Grandpont is a Victorian development, built just south of the river. It had previously been used as a rubbish tip, but needs must. As a resident of Newton Road, writing in my attic room, I looked out and decided my Detective Inspector Susan Holden would live within my sight so I could keep an eye on her. So, if you walk up Edith Road and then follow it round on to Chilswell Road, there on your left, tucked away in a row of terraced houses, is where Detective Inspector Holden lives. But don't go knocking on any doors there, because she is a fiction, and even if she wasn't, she's famously aggressive and would very likely give you an earful for bothering her.

She has enough trouble from her mother, who lives at the far end of the road in Grandpont Grange. As anyone local will tell you, this is in fact Pegasus Grange, built as retirement flats on the former site of Oxford City FC.

> 'Had a late night, my dear?' beamed her mother. Susan Holden, who was expecting a verbal barrage on the importance of punctuality and the neglect of the elderly by the younger generation, was taken completely off guard. The woman looked like her mother. She dressed like her mother. She was even wearing her mother's favourite perfume.
>
> 'Lucky you,' the imposter continued. 'If I were twenty years younger, I'd be out there clubbing with you!'
>
> Holden, who at the age of 32 considered herself long retired from the clubbing scene, grinned at the improbable thought of her morphed mother and herself at the Park End. 'Mmm, I smell coffee,' she said, as she pulled her shoes off in the hall, and placed them tidily in the corner.
>
> 'It's been ready for ten minutes, actually' her mother said firmly, as if to remind her daughter that she had not a personality change.

'Sorry I'm late.' The words came out automatically, and the Detective Inspector was a little girl again, failing to meet the expected standards.

6. St Matthew's Church, Marlborough Road, OX1 4LW

Last stop on the walk is St Matthew's Church, in Marlborough Road. Consecrated in 1890, it has virtually no stained glass, a spacious interior – and I have attended it for many years. In my fictional world, it has been renamed as St Mark's. In *Dead in the Water*, two members of the congregation end up dead, so is it a fellow worshipper who dunnit? Private eye Mullen finds himself forced to go to a service there, and finds himself in an alien environment.

> It was, by Mullen's reckoning, thirty seconds after the official start time of the ten-thirty service, but the vicar – low key in blue clerical blouse and collar, plus darker blue skirt with matching sandals – was showing no signs of getting things started. Two old ladies sitting at the front had turned round and were staring at him, as if he was the major attraction of the zoo. Mullen tried not to mind. Everyone seemed to be wanting to get a look at him. Was that because he was new or because word had got around about who he was?

There is plenty more to Grandpont. At the end of Whitehouse Road, go for a walk in Grandpont Nature Park, before going over the Gasworks Bridge and along the path by a tributary which will lead you to the Westgate Centre. Enjoy the views across Oxford: a city of old and new, town and gown.

Appendix

Illustrations

All maps specially drawn for this book by Sebastian Ballard. His copyright.

P. 11 Cover: *Morse, Lewis, Endeavour and Oxford: Celebrating 35 years on Screen*, edited by John Mair, Richard Lance Keeble and Heidi Boon Rickard, London: Bite-Sized Books, 2021.

P. 12 Cover: Cara Hunter, *Close to Home*, Penguin, 2019.

P. 19 Philip Pullman, *The Amber Spyglass: His Dark Materials*, David Fickling Books, 2018

P. 25 Film poster: *Harry Potter and The Philosopher's Stone*. Warner Bros.

P. 35 P. D. James, *A Taste of Death*, Faber & Faber, 1986.

P. 40 Cover: Iris Murdoch, *The Sea, The Sea*, Triad Books, 1980.

P. 47 Catalogue cover: *Lawrence of Oxford*, Magdalen College, 2018.

P. 50 Lawrence bronze plaque: site of City of Oxford High School for Boys.

P. 55 *Alice's Adventures in Wonderland*, Penguin Books, 2012.

P. 67 Cover: Peter Tickler, *Blood on the Cowley Road*, Joffe Books, 2019

Why not sign up to our mailing list here:

Why not browse our BOOKSHOP?

Find out more about Bite-Sized Books here:

Printed in Great Britain
by Amazon